Strategic Studies Institute
and
U.S. Army War College Press

STATE COLLAPSE, INSURGENCY, AND COUNTERINSURGENCY: LESSONS FROM SOMALIA

J. Peter Pham

November 2013

*****

*****

Comments pertaining to this report are invited and should be forwarded to: Director, Strategic Studies Institute and U.S. Army War College Press, U.S. Army War College, 47 Ashburn Drive, Carlisle, PA 17013-5010.

*****

FOREWORD

For almost a generation, Somalia has been a byword for state failure, defying the combined efforts of diplomats and soldiers to restore some semblance of order, to say nothing of a functional national government. In the absence of an effective sovereign, the country is a backdrop for multiple humanitarian crises, as well as the emergence of an epidemic of maritime piracy that threatened vital sea lanes in the Gulf of Aden and the western Indian Ocean. Even worse, notwithstanding a military intervention by the army of neighboring Ethiopia and the subsequent deployment of an African Union force operating with a mandate from the United Nations Security Council, an al-Qaeda-linked militant group, al-Shabaab, managed to seize control of most of central and southern Somalia and confined the internationally-recognized government and the peacekeepers protecting it to little more than a few besieged districts in the capital of Mogadishu.

Consequently, in the space of months, the tide was turned against the insurgents, and a new Somali authority, appointed in late 2012, presents what appears to be the most promising chance for a permanent government in recent memory. It is not surprising that many policymakers have sought to tease out lessons from the apparent success of the "Somali model" that might be applicable to similar situations, both in Africa and beyond, where weak governments face Islamist insurgents, including the Sahel, in particular where al-Qaeda-affiliated fighters and their allies have posed severe challenges to embattled governments.

In this monograph, however, Dr. J. Peter Pham adopts a different approach. Beginning with a keen appreciation for the intricacies of Somali culture and history, he argues that the key is to understand political legitimacy among the Somali and then examines how both al-Shabaab and the different local polities that have emerged in Somalia have, to varying degrees, acquired it—as well as how successive Somali regimes have not. He also explores how weakness of, and divisions among, the insurgents can be better exploited by engaging and empowering alternative centers of legitimacy. What emerges from his analysis is a rather nuanced picture of the counterinsurgency strategy that, following several frustrating years, finally achieved its objectives, as well as several provocative suggestions.

For these reasons, the Strategic Studies Institute is pleased to offer this monograph as a contribution to not only regional knowledge about the social, political, and security challenges faced in a geo-strategically sensitive part of the African continent, but also the broader literature on insurgency and counterinsurgency.

DOUGLAS C. LOVELACE, JR.
Director
Strategic Studies Institute and
U.S. Army War College Press

ABOUT THE AUTHOR

J. PETER PHAM is Director of the Africa Center at the Atlantic Council in Washington, DC. Previously, he was tenured Associate Professor of Justice Studies, Political Science, and African Studies at James Madison University in Harrisonburg, VA, where he directed the Nelson Institute for International and Public Affairs. He has also regularly lectured at the Foreign Service Institute, the Joint Special Operations University, the Defense Institute of Security Assistance Management, and other U.S. Government professional education institutions. Dr. Pham has testified before the U.S. Congress on a number of occasions and conducted briefings or consulted for U.S. and foreign governments as well as private firms. In May 2008, at the invitation of General William Ward, he gave the keynote address at the first Senior Leaders Conference of the United States Africa Command (AFRICOM) in Mainz, Germany, and subsequently served on AFRICOM's Senior Advisory Group. Dr. Pham is the incumbent Vice President of the Association for the Study of the Middle East and Africa (ASMEA), an academic organization chaired by Professor Bernard Lewis representing over 1,300 scholars of Middle Eastern and African Studies at more than 300 colleges and universities in the United States and overseas. He regularly appears in numerous national and international media outlets. Dr. Pham is also Editor in Chief of ASMEA's flagship *Journal of the Middle East and Africa*. A specialist on U.S. foreign and defense policy, African politics and security, and terrorism and political violence, Dr. Pham is the author of over 300 essays and reviews and the author, editor, or translator of over a dozen books — most recently, *Somalia: Fixing Africa's Most Failed State*, co-authored with Greg Mills and David Kilcullen.

SUMMARY

For more than 2 decades, Somalia has been the prime example of a collapsed state, thus far resisting no fewer than 15 attempts to reconstitute a central government, while the 16th such undertaking, the current internationally-backed but struggling regime of the "Federal Republic of Somalia," just barely maintains a token presence in the capital and along the southeastern littoral — and that due only to the presence of a more than 17,000-strong African Union peacekeeping force. In fact, for much of the period, insurgents spearheaded by the *Harakat al-Shabaab al-Mujahideen* (Movement of Warrior Youth, al-Shabaab), a militant Islamist movement with al-Qaeda links, dominated wide swathes of Somali territory and operated more or less freely in other areas not under their de facto control. Despite the desultory record, the apparent speedy collapse of the insurgency since late-2011 has made it fashionable within some political and military circles to cite the "Somalia model" as a prescription for other conflicts in Africa, including the fight in Mali against al-Qaeda in the Islamic Maghreb (AQIM) and its allies.

In contrast, this monograph argues that the failure for so long of any of Somalia's successive governmental entities to prevail over their opponents and bring an end to conflict has little to do with the lack of outside assistance, especially of the military variety, often cited by way of explanation and more to do with other factors on which external actors can have little positive effect. Specifically, if the regime fighting an insurgency is unable or unwilling to take the steps to achieve internal political legitimacy, no outside intervention will be able to help it to "victory." In examining how such has been the case in Somalia, the nature of political legitimacy in Somali society is closely examined, deriving pointers not only from the success of al-Shabaab and its allies, but also those of relatively stable new polities that have emerged in various parts of the former Somali state in mobilizing clan loyalties and local community sensibilities. Both the implications of engaging these alternative centers of legitimacy — an approach the international community only reluctantly and hesitantly came around to embracing — and the potential to exploit the opportunity presented by the weakness of and divisions among the extremists to not only clear a space for humanitarian action, but also to ensure a modicum of stability and security in the geopolitically sensitive Horn of Africa, are then discussed.

Among the lessons thus drawn, which are applicable to other insurgency and conflict situations in Africa, is that the repeated failure of internationally-backed attempts to reestablish a national government in Somalia underscores the limitations of top-down, state-centric processes that are structurally engineered with a bias in favor of centralization, rather than bottom-up, community-based approaches better adapted to the local sensibilities.

STATE COLLAPSE, INSURGENCY, AND COUNTERINSURGENCY: LESSONS FROM SOMALIA

J. Peter Pham

Introduction.

It has been 2 decades since the day in late January 1991 when dictator Muhammad Siyad Barre packed himself inside the last functioning tank belonging to his once-powerful military and ignominiously fled Mogadishu. He left behind a capital in ruins. Caught in the throes of uncontrolled street violence, Somalia has been the prime example of what Robert Rotberg has termed a "collapsed state": a "rare and extreme version of the failed state" that is "a mere geographical expression, a black hole into which a failed polity has fallen," where:

> there is dark energy, but the forces of entropy have overwhelmed the radiance that hitherto provided some semblance of order and other vital political goods to the inhabitants (no longer the citizens) embraced by language or ethnic affinities or borders.[1]

The country has stubbornly resisted no fewer than 15 attempts to reconstitute a central government, and the 16th such undertaking, the internationally-backed,[2] but struggling regime of the Federal Republic of Somalia (FRS), barely manages to maintain a token presence in the capital and along parts of the southeastern littoral—and that much only thanks to the presence of the more than 17,000 predominantly Ugandan, Burundian, and Kenyan troops that make up the African Union Mission in Somalia (AMISOM).[3]

1

For a number of years, insurgents spearheaded by the *Harakat al-Shabaab al-Mujahideen* (Movement of Warrior Youth, al-Shabaab), a militant Islamist movement that was declared a "specially designated global terrorist" by the U.S. State Department in 2008,[4] a "listed terrorist organization" by the Australian government the following year,[5] a "proscribed organization" by the British government in its 2010 Terrorism Act,[6] and a "listed terrorist group" by the Canadian government,[7] dominated wide swathes of Somali territory and operated more or less freely in other areas not under their de facto control—with the exception of the Somaliland and Puntland regions, which will be discussed later. In fact, if the insurgents suddenly suffered several major reverses beginning in 2011, the explanation would seem to lie more with the effects of the drought that struck that year—and to their contribution to and poor management of the resulting famine—as well as the splintering within al-Shabaab ranks, than to any significant battlefield losses by the group.

Nevertheless, the apparent speedy collapse of the insurgency has made it fashionable within political and military circles to cite the "Somalia model" as a prescription for other conflicts in Africa, including the fight in Mali against al-Qaeda in the Islamic Maghreb (AQIM) and its allies. General Carter F. Ham, then-commander of the United States Africa Command (US-AFRICOM), hailed the performance of African militaries in Somalia as "extraordinary," noting that "they really have degraded the capability of al-Shabaab," which was "really diminished . . . because of the role of the Africans."[8] In his valedictory address, retiring Assistant Secretary of State for African Affairs Johnnie Carson celebrated that "one of Africa's most enduring, intractable, and seemingly hopeless conflicts" has been transformed "into a major success story and a potential model for the resolution of other conflicts on the continent."[9] For his part, Michael A. Sheehan, Assistant Secretary of Defense for Special Operations and Low-Intensity Conflict, has declared, "You can see in our strategies, our policies and programs in [Somalia], some of the components of how our strategy might look in the months and years ahead."[10]

In contrast, this monograph argues that the failure for so long of any of Somalia's successive governmental entities to prevail over their opponents and bring an end to conflict has little to do with the lack of outside assistance, especially of the military variety, and more to do with other factors on which external actors can have little positive effect. Specifically, if the regime fighting an insurgency is unable or unwilling to take the steps to achieve internal political legitimacy, no outside intervention will be able to help it to "victory," as even a cursory review of the relationship between legitimacy and military force in civil wars will confirm. In examining how such has been the case in Somalia, it will also be necessary to look at the nature of political legitimacy in Somali society, deriving pointers from not only the Islamist insurgents of al-Shabaab and their allies, but also the successes of relatively stable new polities that have emerged in various parts of the former Somali state in mobilizing clan loyalties and local community sensibilities. Both the implications of engaging these alternative centers of legitimacy—an approach the international community only reluctantly and hesitantly came around to embracing—and the potential to exploit the opportunity presented by the weakness of and divisions among the extremists are then discussed, thus not only clearing a space for humanitarian action, but also ensuring a modicum of stability and security in the geopolitically sensitive Horn of Africa. Finally, lessons are drawn that might have more realistic applicability to other insurgency and conflict situations in Africa.

Identity and Legitimacy among the Somali.

Somali identity is historically rooted in paternal descent (*tol*), which is meticulously memorialized in genealogies (*abtirsiinyo*, reckoning of ancestors) and determines each individual's exact place in society. At the apices of this structure are the "clan-families." According to the most generally accepted division, the major "clan-families" among the Somali are the Darod, Dir, Hawiye, Isaq, Digil, and Rahanweyn. The first four, historically predominantly nomadic pastoralists, are identified as "noble" (*bilis*) clans, while the Digil and Rahanweyn, also known collectively as "Digil Mirifle," were traditionally cultivators and agro-pastoralists and occupy a second tier in Somali society. The latter also speak a dialect of Somali, *af-maymay*, which is so distinct from the *af-maxaa* dialect of the former that it is "properly a not-mutually-intelligible language."[11] A third tier also exists in this Somali social hierarchy, consisting of minority clans whose members, known collectively as *Sab*, historically carried out occupations such as metalworking and tanning that rendered them ritually unclean in the eyes of the nomadic "noble clans."[12] This social hierarchy likewise has implications for political life. It is noteworthy, for example, that the vice president and defense minister (and sometimes prime minister) in Siyad Barre's regime, Mohamed Ali Samantar, was a Sab of metalworking background (*Tumal*). This particular individual who, thanks to a potentially far-reaching unanimous 2010 decision by the U.S. Supreme Court,[13] is currently the defendant in a lawsuit in the U.S. federal courts brought under the Torture Victim Protection Act of 1991 on behalf of victims of the regime. This undoubtedly was related to the fact that his origins made it highly unlikely that he could ever lead a coup against his benefactor.

Because these genealogical groupings have traditionally been too large and too widely dispersed to act as politically cohesive units—although in modern times, the advent of instantaneous mass communications has rendered the segmentary solidarity of their members a significant factor in national politics—the clan-families are now subdividing into clans and sub-clans by descent in the male line from an eponymous ancestor at the head of each clan lineage. Within the clan, the most clearly defined subsidiary group is an individual's "primary lineage," which also represents the limits of exogamy, and within which an individual's primary identification is with what has been described as the "diya-paying group" (from the Arabic *diya*, "blood-wealth"). This most basic and stable unit of Somali social organization consists of kinsmen with collective responsibility for one another with respect to exogenous actors. The unity of the group is founded not only on shared ancestry traced to a common ancestor four to eight generations back, but also on a formal political contract (*heer*) between its members. If a member of a diya-paying group kills or injures someone outside the group, the members of his group are jointly responsible for that action and will collectively undertake the task of making reparation. Conversely, if one of its members is injured or killed, the diya-paying group will either collectively seek vengeance or share in whatever compensation may be forthcoming. Of course, the nature of the clan system is itself very nuanced and, while rooted in blood relationships, is also historically a consequence of nomadic pastoral life, with its need to defend scarce resources, that results over time in an openness to the formation of new alliances and, even later, of new identities.[14] British anthropologist I. M. Lewis, arguably the foremost living authority on Somali history and culture, has observed that:

> the vital importance of this grouping, in an environment in which the pressure of population on sparse environmental resources is acute, and where fighting over access to water and pasture is common, can hardly be overemphasized

since it is:

> upon his diya-paying group, and potentially on wider circles of clansmen within his clan-family, that the individual ultimately depends for the security of his person and property.[15]

The pervasiveness of the clan system distinguished Somalia from the vast majority of post-independence African states, where the principal problem was the formation of a viable transcendent nationalism capable of uniting widely divergent ethnic groups who found themselves grouped together in "states" created by colonialism. The Somali were different. They consisted of a single ethnic group with only one major internal division—the divide that separated the members of the four "noble clans" and the Digil Mirifle—and "considered themselves bound together by a common language, by an essentially nomadic pastoral culture, and by the shared profession of Islam."[16] Nationalism was already part of their experience insofar as national culture is concerned, since they "spoke the same language, shared the same predominantly nomadic herding culture, and were all adherents of Sunni Islam with a strong attachment to the Sufi brotherhood"; all they lacked was political unity at the level of the culturally defined nation.[17] Thus, Somalis formed an ethnic group or nation but not, traditionally, a single polity. Despite 50 years of state-building, urbanization, civil war, state collapse, and emigration, the bonds of kinship remain the most durable feature of Somali social, political, and economic life. While ethnicity is a category that has applicability vis-à-vis non-Somalis, within Somali society, clan is the focus of identity, notwithstanding the fact that the latter, unlike the former, does not exhibit readily apparent formal "markers" but relies instead on genealogical criteria, which, until fairly recently, were orally transmitted.

From Union to Fragmentation: A Brief History of Modern Somalia.

Modern Somalia itself, which historically had never been a unified political entity, was born out of a union between the British Protectorate of Somaliland, which became the independent state of Somaliland on June 26, 1960, and the territory then administered by Italy as a United Nations (UN) trust that had, before World War II, been an Italian colony (*Somalia Italiana*). The latter received its independence on July 1, 1960, and the two states, under the influence of the sort of African nationalism fashionable during the period, entered into a union, even though they had never developed a common sense of nation-hood and had very different colonial experiences, common language and religion notwithstanding. Consequently, by the time army commander Siyad Barre seized power in October 1969:

> it had become increasingly clear that Somali parlia-mentary democracy had become a travesty, an elab-orate, rarefied game with little relevance to the daily challenges facing the population.[18]

A year after taking over, Siyad Barre proclaimed the "Somali Democratic Republic" officially a Marx-ist state and tried to stamp out clan identity as an anachronistic barrier to progress that ought to be re-placed by nationalism and "Scientific Socialism." The non-kinship term *jaalle* ("friend" or "comrade") was introduced to replace the traditional term of polite address *ina'adeer* ("cousin"). The positions of tradi-tional clan elders were abolished or, at the very least, subsumed into the bureaucratic structure of the state. At the height of the campaign, it became a criminal offense to even refer to one's own or anoth-er's clan identity.[19] Given how deeply rooted the clan identity was, it was not surprising that *Jaalle* Siyad Barre failed in his efforts to efface the bonds. Ironi-cally, he evolved over time from a Soviet client into a U.S. ally after President Jimmy Carter broke with the Ethiopian regime of Mengistu Haile Mariam over the latter's increasingly repressive human rights record.[20] Ultimately, the regime itself simply dissolved in January 1991, when Siyad Barre was caught between popular rebellions led by the Isaq and Darod in the north and a Hawiye uprising in central Somalia and chased out of Mogadishu altogether. By the time of the dictator's flight, Somalia had fallen apart into the traditional clan and lineage divisions that, in the absence of other forms of law and order, alone offered some degree of security. The general situation now vividly recalled the descriptions of Richard Francis Burton and other 19th century European explorers: a land of clan (and clan segment) republics where the would-be traveler needed to secure the protection of each group whose territory he sought to traverse.[21]

Although Siyad Barre had adopted "Scientific Socialism" with the professed goal of uniting the nation by eliminating its ancient clan-based division, the dictator soon fell back on calling on kinship ties in order to maintain power — another example of these bonds' continuing relevance. With the exception of his previously mentioned defense chief Samantar, Siyad Barre's most trusted ministers came from his own Darod clan-family: the Marehan clan of his paternal relations; the Dhulbahante clan of his son-in-law Ahmed Suleiman Abdulle, who headed the notorious National Security Service; and the Ogaden clan of his maternal kin. Siyad Barre's "MOD" coalition first led him into the disastrous Ogaden War (1977–78), a clumsy attempt to exploit the chaos of the Ethiopian Revolution to seize the eponymous territory in the Haud plateau that the dictator's irredentist kinsfolk viewed as "Western Somalia." The influx of over a million Ogadeni refugees following the Somali military's humiliating defeat at the hands of the Ethiopians and their Soviet and Cuban allies created enormous problems for the Somali state. These challenges were only exacerbated when half of the Ogadeni refugees were placed in refugee camps in the middle of the northern regions of Somaliland, the historical territory of their traditional rivals, the Isaq. This led to the formation of the Somali National Movement (SNM) by the Isaq. Another result of the failed war was an abortive coup attempt by disaffected officers from the Majeerteen clan, another Darod group; those who escaped arrest went on to form the Somali Salvation Democratic Front, with the backing of their clansmen. Over the next decade, the two new opposition groups, both born of a conflict that had its origins in Siyad Barre's own complicated political management strategy, would light the fuses that would ultimately explode not just the dictatorship, but the Somali state itself.[22]

After the collapse of the Siyad Barre regime, the Hawiye leaders whose forces held sway over the abandoned capital, Muhammad Farah 'Aideed and Ali Mahdi, fell out with one another. The fighting and subsequent cutoff of food supplies brought about a humanitarian crisis that provoked global outrage, leading to no fewer than three successive international military interventions that aimed to secure the flow of humanitarian assistance: the United Nations Operation in Somalia I (UNOSOM I, April–December 1992), the U.S.–led Unified Task Force (UNITAF, December 1992–May 1993), and the United Nations Operation in Somalia II (UNOSOM II, March 1993–March 1995).[23] Ultimately, however, central and southern Somalia reverted to the age-old pattern of armed clan factions mobilized by powerful figures — referred to by Somalis with the traditional title formerly reserved for battle leaders, *abbaanduule*, and thus quickly dubbed "warlords" by foreign journalists. These factions were sustained by the spoils of conflict, vying with each other for control of territory, and such economic assets as could be found amid the ruins of the collapsed state, including bananas for export.[24]

Meanwhile, in the absence of effective political structures of any kind, Islamic authorities arose in response to increased crime, with *shari'a* being a common denominator around which different communities could organize. As the Islamic legal authorities gradually assumed policing and adjudication roles, those authorities who enjoyed access to greater (that is, external) resources acquired greater influence. It should be noted that, although the Somali traditionally subscribe to Sunni Islam, they also follow the *Shāfi's* school (*madhab*) of jurisprudence, which, although conservative, is open to a variety of liberal views regarding practice.[25] Throughout most of the historical times up to independence in 1960, even though different movements existed within Sunni Islam in Somalia, the most dominant among the populace were the Sufi brotherhoods (*tarīqa*, plural *turuq*), especially that of the Qadiriyya and the Ahmadiyya orders, introduced into Somali lands in the 19th century.[26] While traditional Islamic schools and scholars (*ulam*ā) played a role as focal points for rudimentary political opposition to colonial rule in Italian Somalia, their role in the politics of the Somali clan structure was historically neither institutionalized nor particularly prominent. In part, this is because *shari'a* was not especially entrenched in Somalia: being largely pastoralist, the Somali relied more on customary law (*xeer*) than on religious prescriptions.[27] Hence, Somali Islamism is largely a post-colonial movement that became active in the late 1980s; in the absence of the state's collapse and the ensuing civil strife (and, some authors would add, somewhat polemically, the renewed U.S. interest in potential terrorist linkages in the aftermath of the September 11, 2011, attacks on the American homeland[28]), it is doubtful that militant Islamism would be much more than a marginal force in Somali politics.

Religion's increased influence has been largely a phenomenon of small towns and urban centers, although increased adherence to its normative precepts is a wider phenomenon. Islamic religious leaders have helped organize security and other services, and businessmen in particular have been supportive of the establishment of *shari'a*-based courts throughout the south, which were precursors to the Islamic Courts Union established in Mogadishu in June 2006. Suffice it to say, the Islamists attempted to fill certain voids left by state collapse and otherwise unattended to by emergent forces like the warlords. In doing so, they also made a bid to supplant clan-based and other identities, offering a pan-Islamist identity in lieu of other allegiances.[29]

Contemporaneously, in the absence of anything resembling a functioning state and amid the multiplying divisions of a society returning to clan solidarity as the basis for organization, Islam came to be seen by some Somalis as an alternative to both the potentially Balkanizing clan-based identities and the newly emergent criminal syndicates led by so-called "warlords."[30]

The Failure of the Transitional Federal Government.

Since the collapse of the Somali government and state in 1991, regional and international actors repeatedly have tried to find ways to reconstitute the Somali state by sponsoring lengthy peace processes aimed at establishing a functioning government in Mogadishu.[31] The embattled Transitional Federal Government (TFG) was the result of the 14th and 15th such attempts, the "Nairobi" (or "Mbagathi") and "Djibouti" processes.

The Nairobi Process began in October 2002 under the patronage of the sub-regional Inter-Governmental Authority on Development (IGAD)[32] and with international support, especially from the European Union (EU) and the United States. The discussions were so protracted that it took just over 2 years to establish the TFG using the "4.5 formula." According to this framework, power was to be shared between four of the clan-families—Darod, Dir, Hawiye, and Digil Mirifle (the Isaq, centered in Somaliland, declined to participate)—with some space (the "0.5") granted to minority clans. The Transitional Federal Charter, agreed to in October 2004, gave the Transitional Federal Institutions of government a 5-year mandate. Heading up this structure was Darod warlord Abdullahi Yusuf Ahmad, who launched his national political career with the proceeds of a $1 million ransom he had extracted from the Taiwanese after his militia seized the trawler MV *Shen Kno II* in 1997.

Not until June 2005—and then only under heavy pressure from the Kenyan government, which tired of footing the bill for guests who had long overstayed their welcome—did the TFG finally relocate to Somali territory. Even then, the putative government could not enter its capital—Prime Minister Mohamed Ali Ghedi, who, to his credit, at least made the attempt, narrowly escaped assassination for his trouble—and settled instead in Jowhar, a provincial town safely north of Mogadishu, under the protection of a local warlord who was a fellow Hawiye clansman and patron of the prime minister. When relations with the warlord eventually soured, the TFG was forced to move on and, in a turn of events that is particularly humiliating in the Somali cultural context, take shelter among the Rahanweyn in the backwater of Baidoa, some 250 kilometers southwest of the capital. So undesirable was the location and so reduced the government's circumstances that it was February 2006 before the TFG could muster a quorum to convene its parliament in a converted barn.[33]

Meanwhile, a new force was emerging in Somalia, the Union of Islamic Courts, which was made up of the militias of the various local tribunals set up by the Islamists that took control of Mogadishu in June 2006 after defeating a ragtag coalition of warlords and business leaders hastily thrown together by the United States (presumably acting through the Central Intelligence Agency) under the rather ironic banner of the "Alliance for the Restoration of Peace and Counter-Terrorism." The American intervention achieved the exact opposite of what was intended: far from being checked, the Islamists actually prevailed and, for the first time since the fall of Siyad Barre, Mogadishu was united under a single administration. Moreover, the Islamists, who reorganized themselves into a governmental structure called the Council of Islamic Courts (CIC), quickly extended their control over much of southern and central Somalia, from the southern border of Puntland in the north to the Kenyan frontier in the south, leaving the TFG cowering in Baidoa beneath the cover of a protection force provided by Ethiopia.[34]

The CIC was, in many respects, a mixed blessing for most Somalis. The Islamists cleared away the roadblocks that had been set up by rival militias over the years and reopened the port of Mogadishu. They organized some rudimentary services, including the first municipal garbage collection in nearly 2 decades. On the other hand, these improvements went hand in hand with the imposition of Islamic strictures that were largely alien to the Somali experience, including a ban on watching the 2006 FIFA World Cup (deemed "un-Islamic behavior").[35]

Given their own earlier experiences with Somali Islamism, especially *al-Itihaad al-Islamiya* (the Islamic Union), a group established in the early 1980s that sought to create an expansive Islamic Republic of Greater Somalia and eventually a political union embracing all Muslims in the Horn of Africa,[36] it was not surprising that, after many of the same extremists assumed positions of authority in the CIC, neighboring Ethiopia would be alarmed by the rapid Islamist rise in Somalia. When a CIC attack on the TFG in Baidoa, where the remnants of the TFG were being protected by units from the Ethiopian National Defense Force (ENDF), provided the *casus belli*, Ethiopian Prime Minister Meles Zenawi launched a full-scale military intervention on Christmas Eve 2006. The heavily armed and well-trained Ethiopians quickly routed the CIC's forces, many of whose commanders made the mistake of deploying units in open country, where they were slaughtered by the invaders. "On the coat-tails of the Ethiopian forces rode the TFG"[37] which, with the help of the ENDF expeditionary force, assumed control over key government buildings in Mogadishu.

As the populace's sullen acquiescence to the new regime turned into resentment of what amounted to a de facto foreign occupation, an insurgency gathered steam. Seeming impervious to his increasingly tenuous position, Abdullahi Yusuf was finally forced to resign as president of the TFG in late 2008, with his intransigence increasingly viewed by Somalia's neighbors as an obstacle to the peace process they had launched earlier that year by reaching out to the regime's supposedly "moderate" opponents, led by former Islamic Courts leader Sheikh Sharif Sheikh Ahmed. Sharif Ahmed was himself installed as the new TFG president in January 2009 by an electoral assembly packed for that purpose, which convened in Djibouti under the sponsorship of the Nairobi-based UN Political Office for Somalia and its head, the special representative of UN Secretary General Ban Ki-moon, former Mauritanian politician Ahmedou Ould-Abdallah. The mandate of the new regime was extended until August 2011[38] and then, as that date drew near, until August 2012 in a deal between the TFG president and parliamentary speaker,[39] although the legal authority under which they acted could not be ascertained.

Not surprisingly, given its path to power, the new iteration of the TFG has basically been "unable to expand its authority beyond Villa Somalia in Mogadishu, seat of the presidency" and "had little relevance."[40] In the summer of 2009, when the insurgents attempted to encircle the TFG in Mogadishu, a number of analysts were surprised by the effectiveness of the Islamist push through territory controlled by Sharif Ahmed's own Harti sub-clan of the Abgaal clan—the reluctance of even his closest kinsmen to defend him was a strong indicator of his near-total lack of legitimacy. The promising alliance in early 2010 between the regime and the new Sufi movement, *Ahlu Sunna wal-Jama'a* ([Followers of] the Traditions and Consensus [of the Prophet Muhammad], or ASWJ), whose militias had opposed the Islamist insurgents in the central regions of Somalia, collapsed when Sharif Ahmed reneged on the terms of the power-sharing agreement. Since then, with little reference to the TFG, the various clan militia loosely grouped together under the banner of ASWJ gained control of significant parts of the central Somali region of Galguduud in late-2010 through early-2011 and made modest but appreciable progress toward achieving local security and stability.

Meanwhile, the TFG president became as unwilling as his predecessor to engage in the sort of deal making that would co-opt key stake holders, extend his regime's political base, and possibly prepare the ground for security operations that might break the continual stalemate.[41] A March 2010 report by the UN Monitoring Group on Somalia was, for a diplomatic document, unusually candid in its assessment of the regime and was, for all intents and purposes, a scathing indictment not only of the TFG, but also of any policy built on it:

> The military stalemate is less a reflection of opposition strength than of the weakness of the Transitional Federal Government. Despite infusions of foreign training and assistance, government security forces remain ineffective, disorganized and corrupt—a composite of independent militias loyal to senior government officials and military officers who profit from the business of war and resist their integration under a single command. During the course of the mandate, government forces mounted only one

notable offensive and immediately fell back from all the positions they managed to seize. The government owes its survival to the small African Union peace support operation, AMISOM, rather than to its own troops....[42]

The security sector as a whole lacks structure, organization and a functional chain of command—a problem that an international assessment of the security sector attributes to 'lack of political commitment by leaders within the Transitional Federal Government or because of poor common command and control procedures.'. . . To date, the Transitional Federal Government has never managed to deploy regimental or brigade-sized units on the battlefield.

The consequences of these deficiencies include an inability of the security forces of the Transitional Federal Government to take and hold ground, and very poor public perceptions of their performance by the Somali public. As a result, they have made few durable military gains during the course of the mandate, and the front line has remained, in at least one location, only 500 meters from the presidency.[43]

In early 2011, the International Crisis Group also issued an indictment of the TFG, declaring that members of the regime were "not fit to hold public office and should be forced to resign, isolated, and sanctioned."[44] The document bemoaned the fact that the TFG "has squandered the goodwill and support it received and achieved little of significance in the 2 years it has been in office," and that "every effort to make the administration modestly functional has become unstuck."[45] This harsh assessment was echoed by the judgment in the most recent report of the UN Monitoring Group, released by the Security Council in July 2011:

The principal impediments to security and stabilization in southern Somalia are the Transitional Federal Government leadership's lack of vision or cohesion, its endemic corruption and its failure to advance the political process. Arguably even more damaging is the Government's active resistance to engagement with or the empowerment of local, de facto political and military forces elsewhere in the country. Instead, attempts by the Government's leadership to monopolize power and resources have aggravated frictions within the transitional federal institutions, obstructed the transitional process and crippled the war against Al-Shabaab, while diverting attention and assistance away from positive developments elsewhere in the country.[46]

Moreover, international efforts to bolster the regime proved not only ineffective, but also counterproductive. A review of the TFG's books for the years 2009 and 2010 revealed that although bilateral assistance to the regime during this period totaled $75,600,000, only $2,875,000 could be accounted for. The regime's auditors — imposed by representatives of weary donors, especially the European Commission's special envoy to Somalia, Belgian diplomat George-Marc André — determined that the missing money, which represents more than 96 percent of direct international aid to the TFG, was simply "stolen" and specifically recommended forensic investigations of the Office of the President, the Office of the Prime Minister, the Ministry of Finance, and the Ministry of Telecommunications, the most egregious offenders.[47] Out of the roughly 9,000 troops that the three separate military missions headed by the United States, the EU, and France have trained and armed for the regime, no more than 1,000 remained in Somalia.[48] Efforts to supply this miniscule force actually increased the threat to regional security, with the UN Monitoring Group citing reports that between one-third and one-half of armaments supplied to the regime ended up in the illicit market and concluding that:

> diversion of arms and ammunition from the Transitional Federal Government and its affiliated militias has been another significant source of supply to arms dealers in Mogadishu, and by extension to al-Shabaab.[49]

The investigators even highlighted one case in which a rocket-propelled grenade launcher and associated munitions, purchased for the regime under a U.S. State Department contract to DynCorp International, found their way into a stronghold of al-Shabaab that AMISOM captured in early 2011.[50]

AMISOM: Peacekeepers with No Peace to Keep.

Since the TFG "failed to generate a visible constituency of clan or business supporters in Mogadishu," the regime's very survival depended "wholly on the presence of AMISOM forces."[51] The question became whether or not the "peacekeeping" mission was sustainable as a military operation, much less viable as a strategy.

To its credit and that of its international partners like the United States—which indirectly financed the use of private contractors to train, equip, and, in some cases, guide the African troops in operations[52]—the progress made by AMISOM over time was undeniable. Nonetheless, AMISOM's capacity was consistently hampered by its lack of manpower and materiel. It took 4 years for the force to reach its original authorized strength of 8,000 peacekeepers, with almost all the troops coming from Burundi and Uganda.[53] While additional deployments from those two countries in the first half of 2011 brought the total AMISOM troop strength to just about 10,000, there were considerable difficulties in bringing the numbers up to the new ceiling of 12,000 authorized by the UN Security Council in December 2010. Even if the troops had been raised and the international community, acting through the UN, the African Union (AU), or IGAD, been able to adequately equip the enlarged force in an expeditious amount of time, it was hardly realistic to expect that a 12,000-strong contingent would succeed where the infinitely more robust and better trained and armed UNITAF and UN Operations in Somalia (UNOSOM) II forces, with their 37,000 and 28,000 personnel respectively, failed just a decade and a half earlier against a far less capable opposition than the current crop of Islamist insurgents.[54]

In a successful model of counterinsurgency, the 2006–07 Iraq "surge," the United States committed more than 160,000 troops to Iraq, backed by a further 100,000 servicemen and women deployed elsewhere in the region to provide rear support.[55] These numbers translate into one pair of boots on the ground for every 187 Iraqis. AMISOM, in contrast, was tasked with doing much the same job with one soldier for every 500 Somalis—if it limited its ambitions to just southern and central Somalia. AMISOM's problem was, unfortunately, an all-too-familiar one: its political architects gave very little thought to what they hoped to achieve in Somalia, how they intended to achieve those aims, and what their exit strategy might be. Instead, the result has been nothing more than a charade, whereby the international community pretended to be doing something while it really did very little, all the while throwing increasing, but nonetheless inadequate, numbers of African soldiers into a conflict that they cannot hope to win.[56] One of the few factors aside from ideology that unites the various Shabaab factions among themselves was opposition to the TFG and its AMISOM protectors. While instances of the sort of indiscriminate shelling that characterized the TFG's response to insurgent attacks early in the mission have decreased with training, improved targeting, and the identification of no-fire zones,[57] the mere presence of the AU force and deeply ingrained Somali resentment of foreign intervention in the country has enabled al-Shabaab to rally support from a Somali populace that otherwise has little time for its alien strictures, much less its ham-fisted management of the famine.

The Islamist Insurgents.

While the 2006 Ethiopian intervention ended the rule of the Islamic Courts, the latter's al-Shabaab militia not only survived, but later emerged as the dominant force opposing the TFG and its international supporters. Al-Shabaab itself was born earlier under the leadership of one of the CIC's more hard-line leaders, Sheikh Hassan Dahir 'Aweys, who wanted to create a military wing for the Islamist movement whose members would be not only well-trained, but also indoctrinated to a pan-Islamist identity that transcended clan allegiances. Dahir 'Aweys entrusted this initiative to one of his young deputies, Adan Hashi Farah ("Ayro"), who had travelled to and been trained in Afghanistan before the al-Qaeda attacks on the United States and the subsequent American-led invasion in 2001. Other prominent leaders of the group had also had experience in Afghanistan and Kashmir, including Mukhtar Robow Ali ("Abu Mansur"), Ibrahim Haji Jama ("al-Afghani"), and Ahmed Abdi Godane, ("Abu Zubair"), who eventually succeeded Ayro as the group's nominal leader after the latter was killed in a U.S. airstrike in May 2008.[58]

After the Ethiopian invasion destroyed the CIC, al-Shabaab began to operate as an independent entity. Over time, the group—insofar as its various units and factions can be said to share commonalities—has shifted its emphases from a purely local focus on driving out foreign forces to an increasingly international agenda that has produced both a twin bombing in Kampala, Uganda, in July 2010, and formal proclamations of its adhesion to al-Qaeda. Gradually gaining control over much of southern and central Somalia—in January 2009, it even took control of Baidoa, an objective that eluded its former parent organization, the CIC—al-Shabaab has established local governments in those areas that administer its harsh version of *shari'a*, as well as adjudicating more prosaic disputes. Since early 2009, al-Shabaab forces have not only attacked the TFG, but also battled with AMISOM forces, drawing the peacekeepers deeper into the conflict and causing them to suffer increasing casualties from terrorist attacks such as the September 17, 2009, suicide bombing that killed 17 peacekeepers, including deputy force commander Brigadier General Juvenal Niyoyunguruza of Burundi, and wounded more than 40 others.[59] Al-Shabaab has also enjoyed some success reaching out to the Somali diaspora elsewhere in Africa and in Europe, North Africa, the Middle East, and Australia. Although the number of Somali recruits is tiny compared to the estimated two million Somalis in the diaspora, the relative success of the recruitment program has focused considerable international attention—from both terrorist networks and law enforcement officials—on al-Shabaab's capabilities, especially the extremist group's reach into diaspora communities. One young recruit, Shirwa Ahmed, perpetrated what was the first known suicide attack by an American citizen when, in October 2008, he detonated a vehicle-borne improvised explosive device in Puntland. Others in the diaspora have been indicted by U.S. prosecutors for sending funding to the insurgency.[60] Al-Shabaab has also provided training camps for foreign Islamist militants, as well as safe haven for some high-ranking al-Qaeda operatives in East Africa, including Abu Taha al-Sudani and Saleh Ali Saleh Nabhan, who were subsequently killed by Ethiopian and U.S. special operations forces, respectively.[61]

Regarding al-Shabaab and its place among international terrorist networks, considerable confusion and misinformation about the group exists. Most analysts did not believe that al-Shabaab was, for most of its history, a branch of or under the operational control of al-Qaeda.[62] However, most—including the U.S. State Department's congressionally mandated *Country Reports on Terrorism*—acknowledged that there are many links between the two organizations.[63] Certainly, there was evidence dating back to at least 2007 of operational links—including transfers of knowledge and equipment—between al-Shabaab in Somalia and what eventually emerged as al-Qaeda in the Arabian Peninsula (AQAP) in

Yemen. Those same links seem also to be at work in the case of Ahmed Abdulkadir Warsame, a mid-level al-Shabaab militant captured by U.S. forces in early 2011 while traveling between Somalia and Yemen, whose nine-count indictment on terrorism charges by a grand jury in the U.S. Federal Court of the Southern District of New York was unsealed in early July 2011; the evidence obtained from his questioning by the High-Value Interrogation Group is said to have provided some of the clearest evidence to date of a deepening relationship between al-Shabaab and AQAP.[64] So while unlike the other major violent Islamist extremist group in Africa, AQIM,[65] al-Shabaab was never formally admitted as a branch of al-Qaeda during Osama bin Laden's lifetime, its status changed as his successors sought to establish a name for themselves by carrying out attacks—or, at the very least, apparently expanding the network— wherever they could. Thus, in February 2012, al-Shabaab leader Godane released a video announcing the group's merger with the remnant of al-Qaeda headed by al-Zawahiri.[66]

Generally allied with al-Shabaab—although occasionally also competing with it for control of key towns and strategic resources like the port of Kismayo—is *Hizbul Islam* (Islamic Party), formed by 'Aweys and other exiled former CIC hard-liners after the "moderates" acceded to the Djibouti Process with the TFG in 2008. The group's primary difference from al-Shabaab is that it does not place as much emphasis on global jihadist objectives; rather, its two principal demands are the implementation of a strict version of *shari'a* as the law in Somalia and withdrawal of all foreign troops from the country. Although it lost control of the strategic central town of Beledweyne to

25

al-Shabaab forces in June 2010, Hizbul Islam still controlled some territory in the southern and central Somali regions of Bay and Lower Shabelle. Subsequently, during the Muslim holy month of Ramadan, the two groups cooperated on a joint offensive against TFG and AMISOM forces in Mogadishu.

Another insurgent group that has been prominent in Somalia was the Mu'askar Ras Kamboni (Ras Kamboni Brigades), led by Hassan Abdullah Hersi ("al-Turki"), a former military commander for the Islamic Courts. Based in Middle and Lower Jubba Valley, where it gained control of several strategically located towns that control access to the Kenyan border, including Jilib Afmadoow and Dhoobley, the Ras Kamboni Brigades were aligned with Hizbul Islam until the beginning of 2010, when the group announced it was joining forces with al-Shabaab. Subsequently, the two groups proclaimed their adhesion to "the international jihad of al-Qaeda."[67]

Over time, the insurgents' attacks have progressively increased in both ambition and sophistication. For example, whereas the September 2009 suicide bombing of AMISOM headquarters and the December 3, 2009, assault that killed three TFG ministers and 16 people attending a graduation ceremony at Mogadishu's Shamu Hotel, both relied solely on explosives to inflict damage.[68] The August 24, 2010, attack on the Muna Hotel, a location just blocks from Villa Somalia that was frequented by TFG officials, involved al-Shabaab fighters dressed in government uniforms who went through the building, room by room, killing their victims. They then fought incoming security forces for some time before finally detonating their suicide vests.[69]

In the aftermath of its losses in the Ramadan offensive of 2010, al-Shabaab reshuffled its leadership, with Ibrahim Haji Jama, a militant who trained and fought in Afghanistan and Kashmir before returning to Somalia, emerging as the nominal leader of the group. More significantly, al-Shabaab has apparently formally adopted a decentralized system in which various leaders assume command in their home areas where they are most likely to garner support from fellow clansmen: the erstwhile emir Godane assumed control of operations in Somaliland; Fuad Mohamed Qalaf ("Shongole") was put in charge in Puntland; Abu Mansur assumed command of the Bay and Bakool regions of southern Somalia; Hassan Abdullah Hersi ("al-Turki") continued to hold sway over the Middle and Lower Jubba Valley, albeit with greater integration of his Ras Kamboni Brigades into the al-Shabaab organization; and Ali Mohamed Raghe ("Dheere") overseeing Mogadishu with the assistance of the Comoros-born al-Qaeda in East Africa chief Fazul Abdullah Mohammed (until the latter's June 2011 murder).[70] In this respect, the insurgents essentially combined and exploited the advantages of both clan ties and Islamic identities.

The Somalia that Works: "Bottom-Up" versus "Top-Down."

The most damning aspect of the utter failure of the 14 different attempts to rebuild the national-level institutions of the Somali state before the TFG and the struggles of the latter to survive the daily assaults of the Islamist insurgency was the presence of ready examples elsewhere in Somali territory of what is possible when a "bottom-up" or "building-block" strategy is adopted instead of a continual default to a "top-down" approach in conflict resolution, peace building, or counterinsurgency. These examples illustrate how a process that is viewed as legitimate and supported by the populace can also address the international community's interests concerning issues ranging from humanitarian concerns to maritime piracy to transnational terrorism.[71]

Although they differ significantly in their political development and the courses they have charted for themselves, the northern Somali regions of Somaliland and Puntland have both been relatively successful in avoiding not only embroilment in the violence that has consumed most of southern and central Somalia, but also major internal conflict.[72]

After the collapse of the Somali state, elders representing the various clans in the former British Somaliland Protectorate of Somaliland met in the ravaged city of Burao and agreed to a resolution that annulled the northern territory's merger with the former Italian colony and declared a reversion to the sovereign status it had enjoyed after its achievement of independence from Great Britain. Unlike other parts of Somalia, conflict in the region was averted when the SNM, the principal opposition group that had led the resistance against the Siyad Barre dictatorship in the region, and Isaq clan leaders purposely reached out to representatives of other clans in Somaliland, including the Darod/Harti (Dhulbahante and Warsangeli sub-clans) and Dir (Gadabuursi and Ise sub-clans). Chairman of the SNM Abdirahman Ahmed Ali ("Tuur") was appointed by consensus at the Burao conference to be interim president of Somaliland for 2 years. In 1993, the Somaliland clans sent representatives to Borama for a national guurti, or council of elders, which elected as president Mohamed Haji Ibrahim Egal, who had briefly been prime minister of independent Somaliland in 1960, as well as the democratically elected prime minister of Somalia between 1967 and the military coup in 1969. Interestingly, while the apportionment of seats at the two conferences was conducted along clan lines in a rough attempt to reflect the demographics of the territory, the actual decisionmaking was carried out by consensus.[73]

Egal's tenure saw the drafting of a permanent constitution, approved by 97 percent of the voters in a May 2001 referendum, which established an executive branch of government consisting of a directly elected president and vice president and appointed ministers; a bicameral legislature consisting of an elected House of Representatives and an upper chamber of elders, the guurti; and an independent judiciary. After Egal's unexpected death in 2002, his vice president, Dahir Riyale Kahin, succeeded to the presidency. Kahin, in turn, was elected in his own right in a closely fought election in April 2003 — the margin of victory for the incumbent was just 80 votes out of nearly half a million cast, and, amazingly, the dispute was settled peaceably through the courts. Multiparty elections for the House of Representatives were held in September 2005, which gave the president's party just 33 of the 82 seats, with the balance split between two other parties.

Although the report of a 2005 AU fact-finding mission led by then-AU Commission Deputy Chairperson Patrick Mazimhaka concluded that:

the fact that the union between Somaliland and Somalia was never ratified and also malfunctioned when it went into action from 1960 to 1990 makes Somaliland's search for recognition historically unique and self-justified in African political history,

and recommended that "the AU should find a special method of dealing with this outstanding case,"[74] no country has yet recognized Somaliland's independence. This apparent snub, while grating to Somalilanders, has not prevented them from building a vibrant polity with a strong civil society sector.

Left to their own devices, the Somalilanders discovered that the demobilization of former fighters, the formation of national defense and security services, and the extraordinary resettlement of over one million refugees and internally displaced persons fostered the internal consolidation of their renascent polity, while the establishment of independent newspapers, radio stations, and a host of local nongovernmental organizations (NGOs) and other civic organizations reinforced the nation-building exercise. The stable environment has facilitated substantial investments by both local and diaspora businessmen, who have built, among other achievements, a telecommunications infrastructure that is more developed than that of some of Somaliland's neighbors.[75] Coca-Cola has even opened a $10 million bottling plant in Hargeisa.[76]

In this context, one needs to single out the educational sector not only as a bridge between Somalilanders in the diaspora and their kinsmen at home, but also an important impetus for the reconstruction and development of the region. The showcase of this link is Amoud University, the first institution of its kind in Somaliland, which opened its doors in Borama in 1997.

The school took its name from an eponymous high school that was the first institution of its kind under the British Protectorate and had been the alma mater for many distinguished Somalilanders. The university was founded as a modest joint effort by local citizens, who assumed responsibility for the initiative, and their relations abroad, especially in the Middle East, who raised money and sent textbooks and other supplies. The institution opened with just two academic departments, education and business administration—the former because of the dire need for teachers in the country and the latter because of the opportunities it provided for employment in the private sector and entrepreneurship. Even a noted Somali critic of Somaliland's quest for independence has praised Amoud for having "under-scored the preciousness of investing in collective projects that strengthen common values and deepen peace" and "given the population confidence that local resources can be mobilized to address development needs."[77] Subsequently, universities have been established in Hargeisa (2000), Burco (2004), and Berbera (2009), although the latter institution has its origins in an older College of Fisheries and Maritime Management.

Unfortunately, Somaliland's political progress has stalled in recent years as a result of the repeated postponement of presidential and legislative elections beginning in 2008. Based on my firsthand observation, it would appear that while the crisis is home-grown, outside actors, especially the European Commission (EC) and the NGO Interpeace, have exacerbated the situation, however unintentionally. First, the nomination of the National Election Commission (NEC) by the president and the opposition-controlled parliament took longer than expected. Then the government in Hargeisa, the EC, and Interpeace reached an agreement to undertake a new round of voter registration throughout Somaliland that would result in the issuance of a combination voter and national identification card — an admittedly important symbolic goal for a nascent state. Complicating the exercise further, the NEC, with the agreement of Somaliland's political parties, decided that the card would carry, in addition to a photograph of the bearer, biometric data. The whole process only began in October 2008 and was soon thereafter interrupted by the suicide bombings carried out by al-Shabaab. When the process resumed, it was carried out with great enthusiasm and dispatch by both government and donors, so much so that fingerprint data were not collected from more than half of those registered, and multiple registrations clearly took place in a number of localities.

Eventually, an internal compromise worked out in late September 2009 by all three of the region's political parties, with encouragement from Ethiopia and the United Kingdom (UK), postponed the terms of the president and vice president until 1 month after the elections — the date of which was not specified — thus preventing the escalation of the crisis into violence but still not carrying out the elections. While the election problem is rooted in Somaliland's internal politics, the outside actors have done their local partners no favors by backing a process that was highly problematic from the outset and then, in the case of Interpeace, becoming embroiled in the expanded conflict. Fortunately, good sense and some timely mediation by the traditional clan elders won the day, and the internationally monitored presidential election in June 2010 that resulted in the defeat of incumbent Dahir Riyale Kahin, the election of Ahmed Mohamed Mohamoud

("Silanyo"), and a smooth transition between the two—an unheard-of occurrence in the region—reinforced Somaliland's case for the international recognition that has thus far eluded it. As one report by a group of Africanist experts concluded:

> Recognition of Somaliland would be a most cost-effective means to ensure security in an otherwise troubled and problematic region. Moreover, at a time when "ungoverned spaces" have emerged as a major source of global concern, not least in this region of the world, it is deeply ironic that the international community should deny itself the opportunity to extend the reach of global governance in a way that would be beneficial both to itself, and to the people of Somaliland. For Africa, Somaliland's recognition should not threaten a "Pandora's box" of secessionist claims in other states. Instead it offers a means to positively change the incentives for better governance, not only for Somaliland, but also in south-central Somalia.[78]

One of the leading experts on the Somalis has put it in even starker terms:

> For both Somalia and Somaliland, separation is viable in that there is no economic interdependence between them, but an enforced union against the will of the majority would become a serious liability, possibly leading to war.[79]

The Darod territories in the northeastern promontory of Somalia have also demonstrated the success of the building-block model and the wisdom of working with the Somali's deeply ingrained clan identities.[80] In 1998, tired of being held back by the constant violence and overall lack of social and political progress in central and southern Somalia, traditional clan elders of the Darod clan-family's Harti clan—including its Dhulbahante, Majeerteen, and Warsangeli sub-groups—met in the town of Garowe and opted to undertake a regional state formation process of their own in the northeast, establishing an autonomous administration for what they dubbed "Puntland State of Somalia." After extensive consultations within the Darod/Harti clans and sub-clans, an interim charter was adopted that provided for a parliament whose members were chosen on a clan basis and who, in turn, elected a regional president, the first being Abdullahi Yusuf Ahmed, who went on to become president of the TFG in 2004.[81]

Following Yusuf Ahmed's departure for what was to be his disastrous tenure at the head of the TFG, Puntland legislators chose General Mohamud Muse Hersi ("Muse Adde") as the new head of the regional administration. After serving one 4-year term of office, Muse Adde lost a reelection bid to Abdirahman Mohamed Mohamud ("Farole"), who was elected in January 2009 from a field of over a dozen candidates. Unlike Somaliland, which has opted to reassert its independence, Puntland's constitution simultaneously supports the notion of a federal Somalia and asserts the region's right to negotiate the terms of union with any eventual national government. In late 2009, in a sign that secessionism nonetheless is gaining some traction, the regional parliament voted unanimously to adopt a distinctive flag, coat of arms, and anthem.

The region has, of course, become the center of Somali maritime piracy.[82] The towns of Eyl and Garaad in Puntland, together with Hobyo and Xarardheere in central Somalia, have emerged as the principal pirate ports. Analysts believe that senior Puntland officials are abetting the piracy networks — the UN Sanctions Monitoring Group has charged that President Farole and members of his cabinet have received some of the proceeds of piracy[83] — and that the region is moving in the direction of "becoming the pirate version of a narco-state."[84] This development should not be surprising given that in 2008 — a year in which an estimated $100 million was paid in ransom to the pirates operating there — the entire budget for the Puntland State amounted to $11.7 million.[85] Nevertheless, one report by the Council on Foreign Relations suggests the possibility of a "grand bargain," in which Puntland reins in its piracy-inclined citizens in return for political and economic engagement by the international community.

> Development agencies should also seek to create a partnership with Puntland's legitimate business community — probably the only social segment currently strong enough to challenge the pirate networks. The international community could focus on organizing the professional community in Puntland into a professional association, providing capacity-building support, and engaging the group in discussions about what can be done to reduce piracy. A program that explicitly ties development incentives in the coastal zones to antipiracy efforts could effectively mobilize a population tiring of pirate promiscuity and excess.[86]

The problem, of course, is getting members of the international community to actually engage a non-state entity like Puntland and to do so in a consistent and sustainable manner. In 2002, for example, the Puntland Intelligence Service was established with American and Ethiopian assistance, but this organization has focused almost exclusively on counterterrorism, while largely ignoring wider human security concerns. The regular police, however, on those occasions when they have been willing to confront pirates and other organized criminals, have more often than not found themselves outgunned.[87]

In addition to this well-known example, other less-developed political entities are also emerging out of processes currently at work elsewhere among the Somali. In the central regions of Galguduud and Mudug, for example, the local residents set up several years ago what they have dubbed the "Galmudug State," complete with its own website.[88] Last year, they elected a veteran of the old Somali military, Colonel Mohamed Ahmed Alin, to a 3-year term as the second president of what describes itself as "a secular, decentralized state." An analogous process is taking place in Jubaland, along the frontier with Kenya, apparently with the encouragement of that country's government, which wants a buffer zone between its territory and the areas controlled by al-Shabaab in southern Somalia. In April 2011, the state announced that a new autonomous authority, "Azania," had been inaugurated by the TFG's own resigned defense minister, Mohamed Abdi Mohamed ("Gandhi"), as its first president.[89] Meanwhile, another self-declared administration, "Himan Iyo Heeb," originally established in 2008 by Habar Gidir clansmen in central Somalia, north of Mogadishu,[90] has apparently become active again.[91] Similar stirrings are occurring among the Hawiye in the Benadir region around Mogadishu and among the Digil/Rahanweyn clans farther south.

Whatever their respective shortcomings, by leveraging the legitimacy enjoyed by virtue of deeply rooted kinship and geographic bonds—to say nothing of a very personal political consent—traditional leaders in

Somaliland, Puntland, and other Somali regions have managed to deliver to their constituents a relatively high degree of peace, security, economic progress, and rule of law, despite the lack of international recognition or involvement. Put another way, they have combined Weber's "traditional legitimacy" and "legal right" with service provision in order to establish a sustainable political arrangement, "an order beside the state."[92] As counterinsurgency theorist David Kilcullen has noted:

> Somalia is virtually a laboratory test case, with the south acting as a control group against the experiment in the north. We have the same ethnic groups, in some cases the same clans or even the same people, coming out of the same civil war and the same famine and humanitarian disaster, resulting from the collapse of the same state, yet you see completely different results arising from a bottom-up peace-building process based on local-level rule of law versus a top-down approach based on putting in place a "grand bargain" at the elite level.[93]

Vital to Somaliland, Puntland, and other areas' relatively successful efforts to avoid both major internal conflict and embroilment in the violence affecting most of southern Somalia has been the role played by their clans. Traditional clan elders have negotiated questions of political representation in key forums. In circumstances under which elections were impossible, representatives were designated by clan units from among their members through a deliberative process in which all adult males had an opportunity to participate, and decisions were made on a consensual basis. In stark contrast to the TFG process, which emphasizes the individual actor, the resulting social contract is created between groups with deeply rooted legitimacy in kinship and geographic bonds.

Interestingly, another trait that the authorities in Somaliland and Puntland share with each other but not with the TFG in Mogadishu is the fact that they have largely been self-supporting with respect to governmental finances. It has been argued that one of the most significant factors undermining state formation in Africa has been a limited revenue base—that is, a dependence on foreign aid and/or natural resource extraction for revenue. Throughout the world, the experience has demonstrated that taxation as a means of raising revenue not only provides income for the state, but also facilitates a greater cohesion between the state and its stakeholders. In contrast, the virtual absence of taxation in post-colonial Africa has resulted in regimes that are largely decoupled from their societies.[94] From this perspective, it is most telling that the most advanced state-building project among the Somalis has been in Somaliland, where the government collects taxes and license fees from business and real estate owners and imposes duties on the trade in khat, the mildly narcotic evergreen leaf chewed by many in the region, as well as on imports and exports that flow through the port of Berbera. The government of Somaliland has actually adopted a "supply-side" approach by managing to increase revenue by more than halving the rates sales and income taxes (from 12 to 5 percent and from as much as 25 to 10 percent, respectively). Responding to this success, the World Bank has undertaken to train tax officials and the U.S. Agency for International Development has agreed to build 10 inland-revenue centers across the region.[95] Furthermore, the funds raised have been spent in a manner that could hardly be more transparent: the introduction last year of universal free primary and intermediate schooling through the elimination of school fees. Likewise, what is arguably the second most successful state-building exercise is occurring in Puntland, where the reliance on customs duties and an occasional fisheries license is perhaps more remote than direct taxes, but nonetheless requires that the government maintain certain minimum levels of efficiency (yet another reason why revenue flows from piracy, which is centered in Puntland, are so pernicious). In contrast, the TFG and its predecessors have relied exclusively on foreign aid—when they were not stealing it.

Perhaps most important in the context of the rising tide of Islamist militancy in southern and central Somalia is the fact that, as one of the most astute observers of contemporary Somali society has observed, this reliance—especially in Somaliland, but also in Puntland—on the older system of clan elders and the respect they command "has served as something of a mediating force in managing pragmatic interaction between custom and tradition; Islam and the secular realm of modern nationalism," leading to a unique situation where "Islam may be pre-empting and/or containing Islamism."[96] The consequence of the development of an organic relationship between Somali culture and tradition and Islam appears to ensure a stabilizing, rather than disruptive, role for religion in society in general and religion and politics in particular. In Somaliland, for example, although population is almost exclusively Sunni Muslim and the shahāda, the Muslim profession of the oneness of God and the acceptance of Muhammad as God's final prophet, is emblazoned on the flag, *shari'a* is only one of three sources of jurisprudence used in the region's courts, alongside secular legislation and Somali traditional law *(xeer)*. However, given the limited resources of the Somaliland government, Quranic schools play an important role in basic education. Yet alongside these popular institutions stand equally well-received secular charities like the Hargeisa's Edna Adan Maternity Hospital, founded in 2002 by Edna Adan Ismail, the former foreign minister of Somaliland, which provides a higher standard of care than is available anywhere else in the Somali lands for maternity and infant conditions, as well as diagnosis and treatment for HIV/AIDS, sexually transmitted diseases, and general medical conditions. Thanks to this integrative approach, the northern clans have largely managed to "domesticate" the challenge of political Islam in a manner that their southern counterparts would do well to emulate.

Although they were a long time in coming, there have been indications that the international community has finally begun to arrive at the same realization. In September 2010, U.S. Assistant Secretary of State for African Affairs Johnnie Carson announced a "second-track strategy" that included greater engagement with government officials from Somaliland and Puntland, with an eye to "looking for ways to strengthen their capacity both to govern and to deliver services to their people."[97] Likewise, the following month, after long refusing to even acknowledge their existence, the AU's Peace and Security Council directed then-AU Commission Chairperson Jean Ping to "broaden consultations with Somaliland and Puntland as part of the overall efforts to promote stability and further peace and reconciliation in Somalia."[98]

Famine Changes the Game?

The sheer magnitude of the 2011 famine ensured that the humanitarian crisis would have a significant geopolitical impact. While there is blame enough to go around, al-Shabaab was particularly culpable because of the role that its policies and actions played in exacerbating the consequences of the disaster.

While most analysts view al-Shabaab as a far from monolithic organization,[99] its leadership had a history of arbitrarily denying relief organizations access to the areas under its control.[100] In early 2010, several international agencies, including the World Food Program, and NGOs pulled out of certain militant-dominant areas after several aid workers were killed and the group began imposing strict conditions on their remaining colleagues, extorting "security fees" and "taxes."[101] Moreover, because al-Shabaab had been designated as an international terrorist organization by the United States and a number of other countries, funding for UN operations has been restricted, while NGOs have avoided working in areas the organization controls for fear of running afoul of laws against providing material support to terrorist groups.[102]

While fears of leakage from aid are not entirely misplaced, a far more important source of income for al-Shabaab was, in fact, more directly related to the drought and famines—that is, the industrial production for export of charcoal. While people living between the Juba and Shabelle rivers in southern Somalia have gathered charcoal for their own use from the region's acacia forests since time immemorial, it is only in the last few years that production has reached its present unsustainable levels. It is estimated that somewhere around two-thirds of the forests that used to cover some 15 percent of Somali territory have been reduced to chunks of "black gold," packed into 25-kilogram bags, and shipped to countries in the Persian Gulf, which have themselves banned the domestic production of charcoal.[103] In the year before their export was finally embargoed by the Security Council in 2012, the UN Monitoring Group conservatively estimated that up to 4.5 million of these sacks are exported each year, primarily through the port of Kismayo, which has been controlled by al-Shabaab or other forces allied to its cause since September 2008, earning the group millions of dollars in profits.[104] Meanwhile, where old-growth acacia stands once grew, thorn bushes now proliferate, rendering the areas useless to the Somali people, whether pastoralists or agriculturalists (the former graze their livestock in the grass that flourishes where the root systems of acacia groves hold in ground water and prevent erosion, while the latter grow staple crops in neighboring lands as long as there are tree stands holding in top soil), and contributing further to the desertification that is always a persistent threat in a land as arid or semi-arid as Somalia. Thus, it was both simultaneously tragic and ironic that when a heavy rain briefly passed through the region that was formerly the country's breadbasket in 2013, the result was not deliverance, but disaster, as, in the absence of any foliage to help absorb the precipitation, flash floods compounded the misery in several places.

Al-Shabaab also operated a complex system of taxation on residents within areas subject to its domination and imposed levies not just on aid groups, but also on businesses, sales transactions, and land. The tax on arable land in particular has had the effect of changing the political economy of farming communities that previously eked out a living just above subsistence. For example, in Bakool and Lower Shabelle—not coincidentally, the first two areas where the famine was declared—communities once grew their own food and, whenever possible, stored any surplus sorghum or maize against times of hardship. However, when al-Shabaab imposed a monetary levy on acreage, farmers were pushed into growing cash crops like sesame, which could be sold to traders connected with the Islamist movement's leadership for export in order to obtain the funds to pay the obligatory "jihad war contributions."[105]

As if all this were not bad enough, once the famine set in, al-Shabaab leaders alternated between denying the crisis—arguing instead that accounts of hunger were being "exaggerated" to undermine their hold over the populace—and preventing affected people from moving in search of food. Whether it is a formal policy of the group or not, al-Shabaab forces have used force or the threat of force to prevent displaced people from leaving its territory to find help in Lower Shabelle[106] and the Gedo and Bay regions.[107]

For a long time, despite the extremist ideology espoused by its foreign-influenced leaders, which set them outside the mainstream of Somali culture and society, al-Shabaab could present itself as being better (albeit harsher) rulers than the corrupt denizens of the TFG. The brutal hudud punishments its tribunals meted out, for example, may have been utterly alien to the Somali experience, but they represented justice nonetheless and were a better alternative than the chaos and lawlessness that was the experience of many Somalis in the 1990s. Moreover, the group managed to wrap itself up in the mantle of Somali nationalism by portraying the AU peacekeepers as foreign occupiers, and the fact that AMISOM troops were propping up the despised TFG and, in the process, causing civilian casualties made this narrative all the more credible. However, as discussed previously, within the last year, AMISOM has improved its capabilities and managed to lower civilian casualties while pushing al-Shabaab forces back within Mogadishu. In addition, the famine, and al-Shabaab's clumsy response to it, have damaged the movement's already questionable reputation for "good governance." Not only have the effects of famine been exacerbated by al-Shabaab, but also the disaster exposed divisions within the movement, with some local councils and militias expressing a willingness to accept help from outside sources, even as the central leadership continued to spurn it.[108] Furthermore, actions such as the refusal to allow people to escape the famine will sap al-Shabaab of what remains of its popular legitimacy. While there is undoubtedly some risk in sending aid to areas where al-Shabaab operates, it is likely that whatever negative effects may result from the assistance will fall largely on the group as some of its local leaders defect or populations are weaned from their reliance on it.[109]

Of course, if one is seeking to use this opportunity to undermine al-Shabaab, the attempt would be more likely to succeed if a prospect more attractive than domination by the venal TFG was offered to communities just freed from the militants' yoke. For example, on August 6, 2011, weakened by the famine both politically and financially, al-Shabaab abruptly withdrew from Mogadishu under cover of darkness. Although its spokesman insisted that the pull-out was merely for "tactical reasons" and that the group had decided to change its strategy to "hit-and-run attacks," the Somali capital was nonetheless left, for the first time in years, entirely within the potential grasp of the TFG.[110] Instead of seizing the opportunity, however, the regime continued to rule as if nothing had changed. Government troops fired on internally displaced persons lined up to receive corn rations from the World Food Program, killing at least seven people, and then tried to steal the food.[111] Journalists subsequently discovered that thousands of sacks of food aid meant for famine victims were being sold at markets around Mogadishu by local businessmen with connections to government officials.[112]

AMISOM Turns the Tide, al-Shabaab Mutates.

The 2011 famine coincided with the long-awaited progress of AMISOM. At the beginning of that year, at not insignificant sacrifice, the AU force had managed to extend its operational reach to 13 of Mogadishu's 16 districts and, according to its commander, Ugandan Major General Nathan Mugisha, to "dominate" in "more than half of these."[113] The strategic effect was even more impressive in that it meant that about 80 percent of the city's estimated two million people were in areas controlled by the force. Then, during the height of the famine in the first week of August, al-Shabaab announced its withdrawal from Mogadishu. While the combined effect of the famine destroying the militants' hitherto lucrative "taxation" rackets and the populace's growing exasperation with their brutality left al-Shabaab at its weakest point in years,[114] credit is also due to the efforts of Nathan Mugisha and his successor, Major General Fred Mugisha, in adapting their troops to fight a counterinsurgency campaign in an urban setting—and with limited resources at that.[115]

While many of the Ugandan and Burundian soldiers who, until quite recently, made up almost all of the AMISOM force, have experience fighting and even counterinsurgency operations in their own countries, these mostly took place in rural settings, not the urban sprawl of a city like Mogadishu. Early in the mission's deployment, AMISOM was widely criticized for the civilian casualties that resulted from its often ham-fisted response to insurgents who fired from populated areas. Under the new doctrine, the use of indirect fire weapons was curtailed and otherwise limited to depopulated areas, while no-fire zones were established in the most densely populated areas. Moreover, civil-military cooperation units were established to investigate such incidents of civilian casualties, which still occurred. Pre-deployment training for AMISOM troops was also bolstered to include counterimprovised explosive device fighting in built-up areas tactics as well as improved communications and medical instruction. Despite these improvements, AMISOM commanders continued to lack combat aircraft and a maritime capability — the latter a significant handicap, given the control of the port of Kismayo by al-Shabaab.

In October 2011, the conflict dynamic in Somalia shifted significantly with the intervention of Kenyan military forces, ostensibly acting in response to al-Shabaab attacks on Kenyan territory, including the kidnapping of several foreigners, although Kenyan domestic political considerations also contributed to the decision.[116] Shortly after that, Ethiopian forces entered Somalia's Bay, Bakool, and Hiraan regions. While the Kenyan Operation *Linda Nchi* ("PROTECT THE COUNTRY") was literally bogged down for several months, having been initiated in the middle of the rainy season, the pressure it brought to bear on al-Shabaab forces in the south allowed AMISOM to re-new the offensive, capturing territory on the outskirts of Mogadishu, including the strategic "Afgooye Cor-ridor" linking the capital with the eponymous agricul-tural center in the Shabelle Valley. The Kenyan troops formally joined AMISOM in July 2012, although the extent to which they are actually under the operational command and control of the AU forces commanders is uncertain. Three months later, the Kenyans and their Somali militia allies—themselves officially rebranded as Somali government forces—succeeded in forcing al-Shabaab to withdraw from Kismayo.[117]

By early 2012, as al-Shabaab faced attacks on three separate fronts by AMISOM, Kenyan, and Ethiopian forces, a divide emerged between the militant lead-ership.[118] On the one side was a "nationalist" faction consisting of clan-based militia leaders who were mainly determined to oust the TFG and expand the power of their own clans, while on the other was a smaller group of hardliners who, with their foreign supporters, emphasized a transnational jihadist agenda. In February 2012, the latter faction formally affiliated with al-Qaeda. While the merger did little to forestall the loss of Kismayo and the collapse of al-Shabaab's control of wide swaths of southern and cen-tral Somalia, under their new branding, the hardline militants have refocused their efforts on sustaining a protracted asymmetric fight involving hit-and-run at-tacks on AMISOM and Somali government positions, the planting of improvised explosive devices, assas-sinations of government officials, terrorist (including suicide) bombings, and the execution of suspected spies. While such attacks may not be able to shift the tide of the war in al-Shabaab's favor, they "are capable of disrupting enemy forces and preventing the transition to a more stable security and political environment."[119]

Another Somali Government.

The TFG's repeatedly-extended mandate expired on August 20, 2012, by which time the regime was so discredited that its international backers were unwilling to see it continue any longer. Consequently, following the London Conference on Somalia hosted by British Prime Minister David Cameron in February, the TFG set into motion a complicated process whereby a group of elders representing the clans and sub-clans, which all now acknowledged remained the permanent framework of Somali society, were supposed to pick a broadly representative constituent assembly. The constituent assembly, in turn, was supposed to prepare a permanent constitution and give way to a parliament, which would elect the president.

Unfortunately, the process was vitiated from the start, with more than half of the supposed "elders" not being elders at all. The vetting process, which was supposed to weed out puppets of the TFG officials and other imposters — as well as those with a history of violence or lacking basic literacy — was predicated on political rivals serving as a check on each other. Instead, TFG President Sharif Ahmed, Prime Minister Abdiweli Mohamed Ali, and Parliamentary Speaker Sharif Hassan Sheikh Hassan put aside their difference and colluded to pack the elders and, consequently, the constituent assembly.[120] Subsequently, it was widely reported that seats in the new 275-member parliament were put on sale for as much as $25,000.[121]

When the new legislature met on September 11, 2012, under AMISOM's protection at the Mogadishu airport to elect a president, the widely-discredited incumbent, Sharif Ahmed, actually won the largest number of votes from the parliamentarians in the first round and fell just shy of the majority needed for another term in office. In fact, what may have caused his loss of the next round of balloting was his own greed: he was reportedly given $7 million dollars from Gulf sources to buy his reelection and yet, until the desperate second round of the vote, he doled out stingy payments in the $10,000 range to the electors, many of whom, when they learned the sum he had at his disposal, turned on him.[122] Instead, they elected a civil society activist and educator with close ties to the moderate Islamist movement *al-Islah* ("Reform"), Hassan Sheikh Mohamud, to head the "Federal Republic of Somalia" (FRS), the failed state's 16th transitional entity since 1991, with a 4-year mandate.

A Lesson about Legitimacy and the Limits of Military Force in Counterinsurgency.

The failure of successive Somali regimes to prevail over their opponents and bring an end to the 2-decade-old conflict has little to do with the complaints often voiced about lack of outside assistance, especially of the military kind, than other factors over which external actors can have little positive effect. Specifically, if the regime fighting an insurgency is unable or unwilling to achieve internal political legitimacy, no outside intervention will be able to help it to "victory," as even a cursory review of the relationship between legitimacy and military force in civil wars will confirm.

It is a principle that, in civil wars, while military force is vital for insurgents—without it, they pose no threat to the state—it is less important to the governments that oppose them. For the latter, while having capable armed forces and the political will to use them is not unimportant, unless the governments achieve legitimacy, their counterinsurgency operations will ultimately fail. As for the sustainability of any peace, it depends less on a government's military strength than on its ability to convince the population of its legitimacy, deriving just powers from those it proposes to govern and providing them with reasonable opportunities for political, economic, and social development.[123]

At a very simplified level, there are three types of parties in any civil conflict: the core group that supports any given faction, whether high-minded principle or mere material interest; those who support the opposing faction; and those, often in the majority, who are disinterested in or indifferent to the competing claims of the rival factions.[124] The factions contend with each other to convince the disinterested populace of their legitimacy, which has been defined as:

> the belief in the rightfulness of a state, in its authority to issue commands, so that those commands are obeyed not simply out of fear or self-interest, but because they are believed in some way to have moral authority, because subjects believe that they ought to obey.[125]

The classic distinction by Max Weber listed three grounds legitimating any rule: traditional legitimacy ("the authority of the eternal past"), juridical right ("rule by virtue of legality"), and charisma ("the authority of the exception").[126] For a government, the provision of goods and services to the population offers another form of legitimacy, or is at least often the first step to creating a system in which its legitimacy is accepted. Conversely, the failure to meet basic expectations weakens the same claim of legitimacy. For its part, insurgents can use terror to underscore an incumbent regime's inability to protect its own population, thus delegitimizing it. More positively, rebels can garner support and legitimacy from the populace by providing it with the very political and social goods that the government has proven unable or unwilling to supply.

In this context, especially for governments, military power has its limits. While military action can remedy some of the symptoms of diminished legitimacy, force alone cannot restore it. It needs to be recalled that the very existence of an insurgency implies a base of support that, if it does not actively aid the insurgents, at least tolerates them and, in so doing, implicitly denies the government's claim to legitimacy. Consequently, the military components of a counterinsurgency must be carefully calibrated to avoid adding to the numbers of the disaffected and "all actions, kinetic or nonkinetic, must be planned and executed with consideration of their contribution toward strengthening [the government's] legitimacy."[127]

The effect of external interventions, whether to assist governments in defeating insurgents or to merely hasten the end of conflicts, also needs to be carefully weighed since they may actually exacerbate a regime's crisis of legitimacy by drawing attention to its weakness and even making it seem to be but a pawn of the intervening force. Just winning, in purely military terms, "may not be enough and, often, may be a mistake or deflect one from grasping the prize of legitimacy itself."[128]

There is little that a foreign actor can do to buttress an allied regime's domestic legitimacy unless the latter is truly committed to taking the necessary measures to maintain — if not enhance — political, economic, and social development not only for its core supporters, but the disinterested portion of the population as well. If, on the other hand, the government under challenge manages to maintain its legitimacy with these two groups, the rebels will be reduced to struggling just to survive. All of this, of course, requires the commitment of considerable amounts of time and resources. As Henry Kissinger succinctly framed it, while "the guerrilla wins if he does not lose," the regime he opposes "loses if it does not win."[129]

Conclusion.

The 2-decades-old crisis in Somalia may have at its origin the collapse of a "failed state," but blame for the prolongation of its misery could be more accurately attributed to a wholesale failure of imagination on the part of the international community and the local actors beholden to it. First, these parties have focused almost exclusively on southern and central Somalia, continually repeating the mistakes of their successive "top-down" attempts at state-building, while obstinately refusing to even acknowledge the largely positive experiences that have unfolded in other parts of the country.[130] Second, their approach has been almost entirely centered upon the state, while ignoring traditional clan and religious leaders, members of the vibrant Somali business community, and civil society actors — the very people whose efforts have prevented statelessness from degenerating into complete anarchy and disorder. Third, when they do deign to intervene through proxies like the brave but, for the longest time, undermanned and poorly resourced Ugandan and Burundian troops deployed in "peacekeeping" where there was no peace, they expend these scarce resources in the vain attempt to prop up an unpopular regime whose legitimacy, in the eyes of many Somalis, is dubious at best. Rather, they should husband scarce resources to contain the spread of instability and prevent additional foreign fighters and supplies from further fueling the conflict.

The creation of the "second edition" of the TFG at the beginning of 2009 was an exercise in political management that was primarily designed to impose a certain preconceived notion. Since an Islamist insurgency was perceived to be the chief challenge, a supposed "moderate" Islamist was installed at the head of the TFG through the extralegal machinations of a group of *ersatz* parliamentarians designated for that purpose by the representative of the UN Secretary General, doubling the size of the already bloated legislature. As it turns out, Sharif Ahmed's sponsors failed to take into account the clan dynamics and soon learned that the new president would have trouble even rallying his own Abgaal kinsmen. By the end of his first year in office, the TFG president controlled even less of Mogadishu than his highly unpopular predecessor, despite the presence of an AMISOM force that was repeatedly reinforced. As he begins what is supposed to be his final year in office, even supporters of the Djibouti Process have publicly cast "an acceptable alternative" to the TFG.[131] In this regard, it would have been helpful if someone had recalled the insight of I. M. Lewis:

If further progress is to be achieved in state-forma-
tion, Somali politicians will surely have to come out
of "denial" and start seriously exploring how clan
and lineage ties can be utilized positively. Perhaps
they could learn from their nomadic kinsmen who
unashamedly celebrate these traditional institutions.
Here a less Eurocentric and less evolutionary view of
lineage institutions by Western commentators, social scientists, and bureaucrats might help to create
a more productive environment for rethinking clan-
ship (i.e., agnation) positively.[132]

Since that advice has not been taken, the international community is left with the inescapable
conclusion drawn from the evidence exhaustively
assembled by the Monitoring Group that about the
only thing the TFG did well was to engage in criminal activity ranging from simple theft of resources
to complex visa fraud schemes. While in its first few
months in power, the FRS, headed by Hassan Sheikh
Mohamud, has shown itself to be considerably less en-
cumbered than its predecessor by allegations of corruption. However, its writ still barely extends beyond
the municipal boundaries of Mogadishu, and its efforts to lift the embargo on the export of charcoal from
Somalia have raised concerns.[133]

A more viable course than the one hitherto adopted by the international community would be one that
adapts to the decentralized nature of Somali society
and privileges the bottom-up approach. The new
course should be better suited to buy Somalis the
time and space needed to make their own determi-
nations about their future political arrangements,
while also being flexible enough to allow their neighbors and the rest of the international community the

ability to protect their legitimate security interests. Supporting governance at the level where it is accountable and legitimate—whether in the context of nascent states like Somaliland and Puntland in the northern regions or in local communities and civil society structures in parts of the south—is the most effective and efficient means of both managing the societal fault lines and countering the security threats that have arisen in the wake of the collapse of the Somali state.

The repeated failure of internationally-backed attempts to reestablish a national government in Somalia underscores the profound error of privileging top-down, state-centric processes that are structurally engineered with a bias in favor of centralization, rather than bottom-up, community-based approaches better adapted to the clan sensibilities of the Somali and viewed by them as legitimate. As one analyst has summarized it:

> The UN, Western governments, and donors have tried repeatedly to build a strong central government—the kind of entity that they are most comfortable dealing with—in defiance of local sociopolitical dynamics and regional history.[134]

This has occurred despite the fact that the contemporary experience of insurgency and counterinsurgency in Iraq and Afghanistan—confirmed by the different outcomes in southern and central Somalia and in Somaliland and Puntland—clearly suggests that bottom-up efforts, especially when they reinforce the connection between legitimate local non-state structures and state institutions, have a greater chance of success. They are more likely to be viewed as legitimate by the populations most directly impacted. The fact is, as one scholar has noted:

> At the dawn of the 21st century, the Somali clans do not appear at all to occupy a place all that fundamentally different from that which they had at the time of colonization.[135]

The stubborn refusal to acknowledge this reality results in the repeated capture of otherwise well-intended efforts by the very spoilers whose lack of legitimacy, originating in their lack of connection to the deep roots of a society's identity, provoked the crisis in the first place. The real tragedy is that the failure to learn this lesson has, in recent years, not only wasted billions of dollars and the lives of hundreds of peacekeepers, but also prolonged the immense human suffering and permitted what is now an al-Qaeda affiliate to entrench itself in one of the most vulnerable corners of the globe. It would be an even greater tragedy if not absorbing this real lesson from Somalia meant that the same error is to be repeated elsewhere in Africa and beyond.

ENDNOTES

1. Robert I. Rotberg, "The Failure and Collapse of Nation-States: Breakdown, Prevention, and Repair," Robert I. Rotberg, ed., *When States Fail: Causes and Consequences*, Princeton, NJ: Princeton University Press, 2004, pp. 9-10.

2. The United States formally recognized the FRS as the country's government in early 2013, a move announced by Secretary of State Hillary Rodham Clinton following a meeting with President Hassan Sheikh Mohamud. See Hillary Rodham Clinton, "Remarks with President Hassan Sheikh Mohamud after Their Meeting," January 17, 2013. The action was significant because while

the FRS's predecessor, the TFG, and the multiple entities before it received various expressions of support from the international community, other states have been reluctant to accord the regime formal recognition. While the United States, for example, never formally severed relations with Somalia after the state's collapse in 1991, it has also never officially recognized any of the 15 transitional governments, through the TFG. For years, the State Department website merely states: "The United States maintains regular dialogue with the TFG and other key stakeholders in Somalia through the U.S. Embassy in Nairobi, Kenya." In fact, the lack of affirmative *de jure* recognition of the TFG is presumed by the introduction in October 2009 of a congressional resolution by the then-chairman of the Africa Subcommittee of the U.S. House of Representatives urging the Barack Obama administration "to recognize the TFG and allow the opening of an official Somali embassy in Washington." The clear implication of this resolution was that the U.S. Government accorded the TFG something less than normal diplomatic recognition as a sovereign state. In fact, this point was formally conceded by the Obama administration in early 2010, when, in a brief filed with the U.S. Supreme Court, the Solicitor General of the United States and the Legal Advisor of the State Department acknowledged that "since the fall of the government, the United States has not recognized any entity as the government of Somalia." Similarly, the British Foreign and Commonwealth Office's website states: "Since the fall of Siad Barre regime in 1991 there have been no formal diplomatic links between the UK and Somalia." See *Mohamed Ali Samantar v. Bashe Abdi Yusuf et al.*, Brief of *Amici Curiae* Academic Experts in Somali History and Current Affairs [Lee Cassanelli, J. Peter Pham, I. M. Lewis, Gérard Prunier, and Hussain Bulhan] in Support of the Respondents, January 27, 2010.

3. In February 2012, the UN Security Council increased AMISOM's authorized strength to 17,731 uniformed personnel, a figure that was reached in December 2012. In November 2012, the Council also added 50 additional civilian personnel to the mission. See UN Security Council, S/Res/2036, February 22, 2012; and idem., S/Res/2073, November 7, 2012. As of the beginning of 2013, the major troop-contributing countries were Uganda (approximately 7,000), Burundi (approximately 5,000), Kenya (approximately 4,000), Djibouti approximately 950), and Sierra Leone (approximately 850). Uganda and Nigeria also each contributed a formed police unit of 140 officers each.

4. U.S. Department of State, Office of the Coordinator for Counterterrorism, "Designation of Al-Shabaab as a Specially Designated Global Terrorist," Public Notice 6137, February 26, 2008, available from *www.state.gov/j/ct/rls/other/des/102448.htm.*

5. Commonwealth of Australia, "Listing of Al-Shabaab as a Terrorist Organisation," media release, August 21, 2009, available from *www.foreignminister.gov.au/releases/2009/fa-s090821.html.*

6. Terrorism Act 2000, Proscribed Organisations, Amendment) Order 2010, No. 611, March 4, 2010, available from *www.opsi.gov.uk./si.si2010/uksi_20100611_en_1.*

7. Government of Canada, Ministry of Public Safety, "The Government of Canada Lists Al Shabaab as a Terrorist Organization", news release, March 7, 2010, available from *www.public-safety.gc.ca/media/nr/2010/nr20100307-eng.aspx.*

8. Carter F. Ham, quoted in Donna Miles, "Ham Reports Progress Against Al-Shabab in Africa," American Forces Press Service, August 22, 2012, available from *www.defense.gov/news/newsarticle.aspx?id=117595.*

9. Johnnie Carson, "U.S.-Africa Partnership: The Last Four Years and Beyond," Remarks at the Woodrow Wilson International Center for Scholars, January 16, 2013, available from *www.state.gov/p/af/rls/rm/2013/202943.htm.*

10. Michael A. Sheehan, quoted in Karen Parrish, "'Small-Footprint' Operations Effective, Official Says," American Forces Press Service, January 31, 2013, available from *www.defense.gov/News/NewsArticle.aspx?ID=119150.*

11. See I. M. Lewis, *Understanding Somalia and Somaliland: Culture, History, Society*, New York: Columbia University Press, 2008, p. 3.

12. See I. M. Lewis, *A Pastoral Democracy*, London, UK: Oxford University Press, 1961.

13. See Supreme Court of the United States, *Samantar v. Yousuf et al.*, June 1, 2010, available from *www.supremecourt.gov/opinions/09pdf/08-1555.pdf*.

14. See Maria H. Brons, *Society, Security, Sovereignty and the State in Somalia: From Statelessness to Statelessness?* Utrecht, The Netherlands: International Books, 2001, pp. 99-113.

15. I. M. Lewis, *Making and Breaking States in Africa: The Somali Experience*, Trenton, NJ: Red Sea Press, 2010, pp. 8-9.

16. I. M. Lewis, "Visible and Invisible Differences: The Somali Paradox," *Africa*, Vol. 74, No. 4, November 2004, p. 492.

17. See I. M. Lewis, *Blood and Bone: The Call of Kinship in Somali Society*, Princeton, NJ: Red Sea Press, 1994, p. 221.

18. Terrence Lyons and Ahmed I. Samatar, *Somalia: State Collapse, Multilateral Intervention, and Strategies for Political Reconstruction*, Washington, DC: Brookings Institution, 1995, p. 14.

19. See David D. Laitin, "The Political Economy of Military Rule in Somalia," *Journal of Modern African Studies*, Vol. 14, No. 3, September 1976, pp. 449-468.

20. See Peter Woodward, *U.S. Foreign Policy and the Horn of Africa*, Aldershot, UK: Ashgate, 2006, pp. 22-27.

21. I. M. Lewis, *A Modern History of the Somali*, 4th Ed., Oxford, UK: James Currey, 2002, p. 263.

22. See I. M. Lewis, "Nazionalismo frammentato e colasso del regime somalo" (Fragmented Nationalism and the Collapse of the Somali Regime), *Politica Internazionale*, Vol. 20, No. 4, 1992, pp. 35-52.

23. See John L. Hirsh and Robert Oakley, *Somalia and Operation Restore Hope: Reflections on Peacemaking and peacekeeping*, Washington, DC: U.S. Institute of Peace, 1995.

24. See Virginia Luling, "Come Back Somalia? Questioning a Collapsed State," *Third World Quarterly*, Vol. 18, No. 2, June 1997, pp. 287-302.

25. Lewis, *Blood and Bone*, p. 167.

26. See I. M. Lewis, *Saints and Somalis: Popular Islam in a Clan-Based Society*, Lawrenceville, NJ: Red Sea Press, 1998.

27. See Michael van Notten, in Spencer Health MacCallum, ed., *The Law of the Somalis: A Stable Foundation for Economic Development in the Horn of Africa*, Trenton, NJ: Red Sea Press, 2006.

28. See, inter alia, Roland Marchal, "Islamic Political Dynamics in the Somali Civil War: Before and After September 11," Alex de Waal, ed., *Islamism and Its Enemies in the Horn of Africa*, Addis Ababa, Ethiopia: Shama Books, 2004, pp. 114-145.

29. See Shaul Shay, *Somalia between Jihad and Restoration*, New Brunswick, NJ: Transaction Publishers, 2007, pp. 93-127; also see Kenneth J. Menkhaus, "Somalia and Somaliland: Terrorism, Political Islam, and State Collapse," Robert I. Rotberg, ed., *Battling Terrorism in the Horn of Africa*, Washington, DC: Brookings Institution Press, 2005, pp. 23-47; and "Risks and Opportunities in Somalia," *Survival*, Vol. 49, No. 2, Summer 2007, pp. 5-20.

30. Abdurahman M. Abdullahi, "Recovering the Somali State: The Islamic Factor," A. Osman Farah, Mammo Muchie, and Joakim Gundel, eds., *Somalia: Diaspora and State Reconstitution in the Horn of Africa*, London, UK: Adonis and Abbey, 2007, pp. 196-221.

31. See J. Peter Pham, "Somalia: Where a State Isn't a State," *Fletcher Forum on World Affairs*, Vol. 35, No. 2, Summer 2011, pp. 133-151.

32. IGAD was founded in 1986 by Djibouti, Ethiopia, Kenya, Somalia, Sudan, and Uganda. Eritrea joined following its independence in 1993 but has since come and gone as a member, according to the state of its relations with its neighbors.

33. See Lewis, *Making and Breaking of States in Africa*, pp. 188-194.

34. See Ken Menkhaus, "The Crisis in Somalia: Tragedy in Five Acts," *African Affairs*, Vol. 106, No. 424, July 2007, pp. 357-390.

35. See Oscar Gakuo Mwangi, "The Union of Islamic Courts and Security Governance in Somalia," *African Security Review*, Vol. 19, No. 1, March 2010, pp. 88-94.

36. See Medhane Tadesse, *Al-Ittihad: Political Islam and Black Economy in Somalia: Religion, Money, and the Struggle for Supremacy over Somalia*, Addis Ababa, Ethiopa: Addis Ababa Publishers, 2002, pp. 16-24.

37. Menkhaus, "The Crisis in Somalia," p. 382.

38. See Ken Menkhaus, "Somalia: What Went Wrong?," *RUSI Journal*, Vol. 154, No. 4, August 2009, pp. 6-12; also see J. Peter Pham, "Peripheral Vision: A Model Solution for Somalia," *RUSI Journal*, Vol. 154, No. 5, October 2009, pp. 84-90.

39. The text of the June 9, 2011, "Kampala Agreement" signed by President Sharif Ahmed and Parliamentary Speaker Sharif Hassan Sheikh Aden and witnessed by Ugandan President Yoweri Museveni and special representative of the UN Secretary General Augustine Muhiga is available from *www.garoweonline.com/artman2/publish/Somalia_27/Somalia_The_Kampala_Accord.shtml*.

40. Apuuli Phillip Kasaija, "The UN-led Djibouti Peace Process for Somalia 2008-2009: Results and Problems," *Journal of Contemporary African Studies*, Vol. 28, No. 3, July 2010, p. 278.

41. See Andre Le Sage, "Somalia's Endless Transition: Breaking the Deadlock," *Strategic Forum*, Vol. 257, June 2010, available from *www.ndu.edu/inss/docUploaded/SF%20257.pdf*.

42. UN Security Council, *Report of the Monitoring Group on Somalia Pursuant to Security Council Resolution 1853*, 2008, S/2010/91, March 10, 2010, p. 4.

43. *Ibid.*, p. 12.

44. *Somalia: The Transitional Government on Life Support*, Africa Report No. 170, Brussels, Belgium: International Crisis Group, February 21, 2011, p. i.

45. *Ibid.*

46. UN Security Council, *Report of the Monitoring Group on Somalia and Eritrea pursuant to Security Council Resolution 1916,* 2010, S/2011/433, July 18, 2011, p. 16.

47. Public Finance Management Unit, Audit Investigation Report Covering Accounting Years of 2009 and 2010, May 2011, p. 3.

48. See Elizabeth Dickinson, "How Much Turf Does the Somali Government Really Control?" *ForeignPolicy.com,* September 23, 2010, available from *www.foreignpolicy.com/articles/2010/09/23/how_much_turf_does_the_somali_government_really_control.*

49. UN Security Council, *Report of the Monitoring Group on Somalia and Eritrea,* p. 43.

50. *Ibid.,* p. 233.

51. Bronwyn E. Bruton, *Somalia: A New Approach,* Council Special Report 52, New York/Washington, DC: Council on Foreign Relations, 2010, p. 10.

52. See Jeffrey Gettleman, Mark Mazzetti, and Eric Schmitt, "U.S. Relies on Contractors in Somalia Conflict," *New York Times,* August 11, 2011, p. A1.

53. Cameroon, Ghana, Mali, and Senegal have sent a token soldier apiece to join AMISOM, while Ghana, Kenya, Nigeria, and Sierra Leone have also sent personnel to man the peacekeeping force's four-dozen-strong police unit.

54. See Jonathan Stevenson, *Losing Mogadishu: Testing U.S. Policy in Somalia,* Annapolis, MD: U.S. Naval Institute Press, 1995.

55. See Steven N. Simon, *After the Surge: The Case for U.S. Military Disengagement from Iraq,* Council Special Report No. 23, New York/Washington, DC: Council on Foreign Relations, 2007, p. 37.

56. See J. Peter Pham, "Somalia: Insurgency and Legitimacy in the Context of State Collapse," David Richards and Greg Mills, eds., *Victory Among People: Lessons from Countering Insurgency and Stabilizing Fragile States,* London, UK: RUSI, 2011, pp. 111-134.

57. See Human Rights Watch, *"You Don't Know Who to Blame": War Crimes in Somalia,"* August 15, 2011, pp. 16-18, available from *www.hrw.org/sites/default/files/reports/somalia0811webwcover.pdf.*

58. See Roland Marchal, "A Tentative Assessment of the Somali *Harakat Al-Shabaab," Journal of Eastern African Studies,* Vol. 3, No. 3, November 2009, pp. 381-404.

59. See "21 Killed in Suicide Attack on African Union Base in Somalia," *CNN,* September 18, 2009, available from *edition.cnn.com/2009/WORLD/africa/09/18/somalia.suicide.attack/index.html.*

60. See Evan Perez, "Case Shows Rise of Non-Bank Transfers to Fund Terror," *Wall Street Journal,* November 17, 2010, available from *online.wsj.com/article/SB10001424052748703628204575618841265233312.html.*

61. Jonathan Stevenson, "Jihad and Piracy in Somalia," *Survival,* Vol. 52, No. 1, February/March 2010, pp. 27-38.

62. See, inter alia, David Shinn, "Al Shabaab's Foreign Threat to Somalia," *Orbis,* Vol. 55, No. 2, Spring 2011, pp. 27-38.

63. See Office of the Coordinator for Counterterrorism, *Country Reports on Terrorism 2010,* Washington, DC: U.S. Department of State, August 18, 2011, available from *www.state.gov/documents/organization/170479.pdf.*

64. See Charlie Savage and Eric Schmitt, "U.S. to Prosecute Somali Suspect in Civilian Court," *New York Times,* July 5, 2011, p. A1.

65. See, inter alia, J. Peter Pham, "Foreign Influences and Shifting Horizons: The Ongoing Evolution of Al Qaeda in the Islamic Maghreb," *Orbis,* Vol. 55, No. 2, Spring 2011, pp. 240-254; also see J. Peter Pham, "The Dangerous 'Pragmatism' of Al-Qaeda in the Islamic Maghreb," *Journal of the Middle East and Africa,* Vol. 2, No. 1, January-June 2011, pp. 15-29.

66. "Al-Shabaab Joining al-Qaeda, Monitor Group Says," CNN, February 10, 2012, available from *www.cnn.com/2012/02/09/world/africa/somalia-shabaab-qaeda*.

67. Abdi Sheikh and Abdi Guled, "Somalia Rebels Unite, Profess Loyalty to al Qaeda," *Reuters*, February 1, 2010, available from *www.reuters.com/article/idUSTRE6102Q720100201*.

68. Stephanie McCrummen, "Bombing Kills 19 in Somali Capital," *Washington Post*, December 4, 2009, p. A19.

69. "Members of Somali Parliament Killed in Bombing Are Identified," CNN, August 25, 2010, available from *edition.cnn.com/2010/WORLD/africa/08/25/somalia*.

70. Abdi Sheikh, "Somalia Says Killed Top African Al Qaeda Operative," *Reuters*, June 11, 2011, available from *uk.reuters.com/article/2011/06/11/uk-somalia-alqaeda-idUKTRE75A12F20110611*.

71. See J. Peter Pham, "The Somali Solution to the Somali Crisis," *Harvard Africa Policy Journal*, Vol. 6, 2010, pp. 71-84.

72. See J. Peter Pham, "The Somaliland Exception: Lessons on Postconflict State Building from the Part of the Former Somalia That Works," *Marine Corps University Journal*, Vol. 3, No. 1, Spring 2012, pp. 1-33.

73. See Mark Bradbury, *Becoming Somaliland*, Oxford, UK: James Currey, 2008, pp. 77-136.

74. African Union Commission, *Report of the AU Fact-Finding Mission to Somaliland*, April 30-May 4, 2005.

75. See Izbal Jhazbhay, *Somaliland: An African Struggle for Nationhood and International Recognition*, Johannesburg, South Africa: South African Institute for International Affairs/Institute for Global Dialogue, 2009; also see J. Peter Pham, "Review of Somaliland: An African Struggle for Nationhood and International Recognition, by Iqbal D. Jhazbhay," *Journal of the Middle East and Africa*, Vol. 1, No. 1, Spring 2010, pp. 139-144.

76. See Sarah McGregor, "Coca-Cola Invests $10 million in Somaliland Bottling Plant," *Bloomberg Business Report*, May 31, 2011.

77. Abdi Ismail Samantar, "Somali Reconstruction and Local Initiative: Amoud University," *World Development*, Vol. 29, No. 4, April 2001, p. 654.

78. Christopher Clapham *et al.*, *African Game Changer? The Consequences of Somaliland's International, Non Recognition*, Brenthurst Discussion Paper, June 2011, available from *www.the brenthurstfoundaton.org/Files/Brenthurst_Commissioned_Reports/ BD-1105_Consequences-of-Somalilands-International-Recognition.pdf*.

79. John Drysdale, *What Happened to Somalia? A Tale of Tragic Blunders*, London, UK: Haan Associates, 1994, p. 148.

80. See Martin Doornbos, "When Is a State a State? Exploring Puntland, Somalia," *Global Forces and State Restructuring: Dynamics of State Formation and Collapse*, New York: Palgrave Macmillan, 2006, pp. 175-194.

81. See Kinfe Abraham, *Somalia Calling: The Crisis of Statehood and the Quest for Peace*, Addis Ababa, Ethiopia: Ethiopian International Institute of Peace and Development, 2002, pp. 445-463.

82. See J. Peter Pham, "Putting Somali Piracy in Context," *Journal of Contemporary African Studies*, Vol. 28, No. 3, July 2010, pp. 325-341; and J. Peter Pham, "The Failed State and Regional Dimensions of Somali Piracy," Frans-Paul van der Putten and Bibi T. van Ginkel, Leiden: Martinus Nijhoff, eds., *The International Response to Somali Piracy: Challenges and Opportunities*, 2010, pp. 31-64; also see Martin N. Murphy, *Somalia, the New Barbary? Piracy and Islam in the Horn of Africa*, New York: Columbia University Press, 2011.

83. See UN Security Council, *Report of the Monitoring Group on Somalia*, p. 39.

84. Ken Menkhaus, "Dangerous Waters," *Survival*, Vol. 51, No. 1, February-March 2009, p. 24.

85. See Brian J. Hesse, "Lessons in Successful Somali Governance," *Journal of Contemporary African Studies*, Vol. 18, No. 1, January 2010, p. 79.

86. Bruton, *Somalia: A New Approach*, pp. 33-34.

87. See Matt Bryden and Jeremy Brickhill, "Disarming Somalia: Lessons in Stabilisation from a Failed State," *Conflict, Security and Development*, Vol. 10, No. 2, May 2010, pp. 251-253.

88. See *www.galmudug.com*.

89. See Richard Lough, "Kenya Looks to Somali Troops, Militia to Create Border Buffer," *Reuters*, August 16, 2011, available from *af.reuters.com/article/topNews/idAFJOE77F0D320110816*.

90. See Ramadan Haji Elmi, "Himan and Heeb—from Hardship to Harmony," *Madasha*, November 2, 2011.

91. "Himan Iyo Heb Calls for Participating in Ending to Inter-Clan Hostilities," *AllAfrica.com*, July 5, 2011, available from *allafrica.com/stories/201107050714.html*.

92. See Dustin Dehéz and Belachew Gebrewold, "When Things Fall Apart—Conflict Dynamics and an Order Beside the State in Postcollapse Somalia," *African Security*, Vol. 3, No. 1, January 2010, pp. 1-20.

93. David Kilcullen, *Counterinsurgency*, Oxford, UK: Oxford University Press, 2010, p. 156.

94. See Jeffrey Herbst, "War and the State in Africa," *International Security*, Vol. 14, No. 3, Spring 1990, pp. 117-139.

95. See Sarah McGregor, "Somaliland Government Plans to Enforce Compliance on Tax, Double Revenue," Bloomberg Business Report, March 31, 2011, available from *www.bloomberg.com/news/2011-03-31/somaliland-government-plans-to-enforce-compliance-on-tax-double-revenue.html*.

96. Iqbal Jhazbhay, "Islam and Stability in Somaliland and the Geo-politics of the War on Terror," *Journal of Muslim Minority Affairs*, Vol. 28, No. 2, August, p. 198.

97. Johnnie Carson, *Remarks to the Press from the UN General Assembly*, September 24, 2010, available from *state.gov/p/af/rls/spbr/2010/147922/htm.*

98. African Union, *Communiqué of the 245th Meeting of the Peace and Security Council,* October 14, 2010, p. 3.

99. A notable exception is Roland Marchal, who has argued that, notwithstanding different conceptions that have been publicly expressed, the group's leadership has maintained a tight control on the apparatus, and that "betting on any splits is an illusion under the current circumstances despite divergent agendas on the military strategy, policies towards the population and attitude in front of the international humanitarian community." See *The Rise of a Jihadi Movement in a Country at War: Harakat al-Shabab al Mujaheddin in Somalia,* unpublished report for H. M. Government, Department for International Development, March 2011, p. 3.

100. See "Ban on Aid Agencies Condemned," *IRIN Humanitarian News and Analysis,* August 10, 2010, available from *www.irinnews.org/report.aspx?reportid=90120.*

101. See Neil MacFarquhar, "Threats Lead Food Agency to Curtail Aid in Somalia," *New York Times,* January 6, 2010, p. A6.

102. See Jeffrey Gettleman, "U.N. Criticizes U.S. Restrictions on Aid to Somalia," *New York Times,* February 18, 2010, p. A8.

103. See "Charcoal Trade Booming Despite Ban," *IRIN Humanitarian News and Analysis,* January 20, 2011, available from *www.irinnews.org/report.aspx?reportid=91679.*

104. See UN Security Council, *Report of the Monitoring Group on Somalia and Eritrea,* pp. 181-184.

105. See Gabe Joselow, "Perfect Storm—Why Famine Hit Southern Somalia First," *Voice of America,* July 25, 2011, available from *www.voanews.com/english/news/africa/Perfect-Storm-Why-Famine-Hit-Souhtern-Somalia-First-1261 19038.html.*

106. Interviews with Somali sources, August 2-3, 2011.

107. Interview with international relief officials, August 18, 2011.

108. See Leela Jacinto, "Famine Weakens and Divides al Shabaab Militants," *France 24*, July 29, 2011, available from *www.france24.com/en/20110729-somalia-al-shabaab-famine-weakens-divides-qaeda-linked-militants*; also see Michele Kelemen, "Opportunity in Famine's Toll on Somali Insurgency," NPR, August 13, 2011, available from *www.npr.org/2011/08/14/139612682/famine-in-somalia-also-taking-toll-on-al-shabaab*.

109. See J. Peter Pham, Testimony before the U.S. Senate, 112th Cong., 1st sess., August 3, 2011, available from *foreign.senate.gov/imo/media/doc/Pham%20testimony.pdf*.

110. See Jeffrey Gettleman and Mohamed Ibrahim, "Rebels Cede Control of Capital to Somali Government," *New York Times*, August 7, 2011, p. A6.

111. See "Gunfire Kills Seven Somali Refugees as Famine Aid is Looted, Witnesses Say," Associated Press, August 5, 2011.

112. See Katherine Houreld, "Somalia Food Aid Stolen, UN Investigating," Associated Press, August 15, 2011.

113. Nathan Mugisha, "The Way Forward in Somalia," *Rusi Journal*, Vol. 156, No. 3, June/July 2011, p. 26.

114. See Bronwyn Bruton and J. Peter Pham, "How to End the Stalemate in Somalia," *Foreign Affairs*, September 30, 2011, available from *www.foreignaffairs.com/articles/68315/bronwyn-bruton-and-j-peter-pham/how-to-end-the-stalemate-in-somalia*.

115. Interview with Major General Fred Mugisha, AMISOM Force Commander, December 6, 2011.

116. Interview with senior Kenyan official, December 3, 2011.

117. "Al-Shabab Rebels Pull Out of Key Somali Town," *Al-Jazeera*, September 29, 2012, available from *www.aljazeera.com/news/africa/2012/09/20129295415328148.html*.

118. See Bronwyn Bruton and J. Peter Pham, "The Splintering of Al Shabaab," *Foreign Affairs*, February 2, 2012, available from *www.foreignaffairs.com/articles/137068/bronwyn-bruton-and-j-peter-pham/the-splintering-of-al-shabaab.*

119. Christopher Anzalone, "Al-Shabab's Tactical and Media Strategies in the Wake of Battlefield Setbacks," *CTC Sentinel*, Vol. 6, No. 3, March 2013, p. 13.

120. Interview with Ambassador Boubacar Gaoussou Diarra, African Union Special Representative for Somalia, July 10, 2012.

121. "Somalia's Government: Baby Steps," *The Economist*, August 25, 2012, available from *www.economist.com/node/21560905.*

122. "Somali MPs Elect Hassan Sheikh as President," *Al-Jazeera*, September 11, 2012, available from *www.aljazeera.com/news/africa/2012/09/201291083927688186.html.*

123. See Eliot Cohen, Conrad Crane, Jan Horvath, and John Nagl, "Principles, Imperatives, and Paradoxes of Counterinsurgency," *Military Review*, Vol. 86, No. 2, March-April 2006, pp. 49-53.

124. See John A. Lynn, "Patterns of Insurgency and Counterinsurgency," *Military Review*, Vol. 85, No. 4, July-August 2005, pp. 22-27.

125. Rodney Barker, *Political Legitimacy and the State*, Oxford, UK: Clarendon Press, 1990, p. 11.

126. Max Weber, "The Profession and Vocation of Politics," Peter Lassman and Ronald Speirs, eds., Cambridge, UK: Cambridge University Press, 1994, pp. 311-312.

127. Cohen *et al.*, p. 50.

128. Timothy J. Lomperis, "Vietnam's Offspring: The Lesson of Legitimacy," *Conflict Quarterly*, Vol. 6, No. 1, Winter 1986, pp. 26-27.

129. Henry A. Kissinger, "The Vietnam Negotiations," *Foreign Affairs*, Vol. 47, No. 2, January 1969, p. 214.

130. See J. Peter Pham, "Somalia and Somaliland: Statebuilding amid the Ruins," Jeffrey Herbst, Terence McNamee, and Greg Mills, eds., *On the Fault Line: Managing Tensions and Divisions within Societies*, London, UK: Profile, 2012, pp. 69-87.

131. See David Shinn, Testimony before the Subcommittee on Africa, Human Rights, and Global Health and the Subcommittee on Terrorism, Nonproliferation, and Trade, Committee on Foreign Affairs, U.S. House of Representatives, 112th Cong., 1st sess., available from *foreignaffairs.house.gov/122/shi070711.pdf*. Shinn, former U.S. ambassador to Ethiopia and onetime head of the Somali office in the U.S. State Department, noted:

> Many in the Somali-American diaspora and a number of American scholars who follow the situation in Somalia have already given up on the TFG . . . . [I]f the TFG continues its internal squabbles and fails to make progress, I may find myself joining this group in August 2012 when there would hopefully be an acceptable alternative.

132. Lewis, "Visible and Invisible Differences: The Somali Paradox," p. 508.

133. See Louis Charboneau, "U.N. Resisting African Calls to End Somalia Arms Embargo," *Reuters*, October 31, 2012, available from *www.reuters.com/article/2012/10/31/us-somalia-un-idUSBRE89U1SZ20121031*.

134. Seth Kaplan, "Rethinking State-building in a Failed State," *Washington Quarterly*, Vol. 33, No. 1, January 2010, p. 82.

135. Christian Bader, *Le sang et le lait: Bréve histoire des clans Somali* (The Blood and the Milk: Brief History of the Somali Clans), Paris, France: Maisonneuve et Larose, 1999, p. 227.

U.S. ARMY WAR COLLEGE

Major General Anthony A. Cucolo III
Commandant

*****

STRATEGIC STUDIES INSTITUTE
and
U.S. ARMY WAR COLLEGE PRESS

Director
Professor Douglas C. Lovelace, Jr.

Director of Research
Dr. Steven K. Metz

Author
Dr. J. Peter Pham

Editor for Production
Dr. James G. Pierce

Publications Assistant
Ms. Rita A. Rummel

*****

Composition
Mrs. Jennifer E. Nevil

* 9 7 8 1 7 8 2 6 6 5 4 0 3 *